Effective Conflict Management

Developing Management Skills

Developing Management Skills

EFFECTIVE CONFLICT
MANAGEMENT

David A Whetten
Kim Cameron
Mike Woods

HarperCollins*Publishers*

This edition first published in 1996 by
HarperCollins College
An imprint of HarperCollins Publishers Ltd, UK
77–85 Fulham Palace Road
Hammersmith
London W6 8JB.

Mike Woods asserts the moral right to be identified as the author of the
adapted material.

British Library Cataloguing in Publication Data. A catalogue record for this
book is available from the British Library.

ISBN 0-00-4990404

Typeset by Dorchester Typesetting Group Ltd
Printed and bound by Scotprint Ltd, Musselburgh
Cover design: The Senate.

Other Titles in the Series

Contents

Preface

Effective Conflict Management is one of a series of six books based on *Developing Management Skills for Europe*, a major work by David Whetton, Kim Cameron and Mike Woods. The other titles from this series are, *Effective Stress Management, Effective Communication, Effective Empowerment and Delegation, Effective Problem-Solving* and *Effective Motivation*. Presented in a convenient form they provide a background of reading and exercises for tutors and students taking MBA grade or other business qualifications.

Each book in the series seeks to find a balance between a sound theoretical background and case studies. Our objective remains, as it did in the combined work, to develop behavioural skills not only to increase knowledge and understanding in the area but also to assist students to apply what they have learned. We hope our readers will be able to achieve their qualifications **and** become productive members of their organisations by learning applicable skills.

The structure of the books and the method of teaching they employ are, in our opinion unique. Each book begins with a series of questionnaires designed to check on the reader's present understanding of the area, and in some cases assist the reader in self assessment. Thus, in the present book, *Effective Conflict Management*, the reader is asked to rate his or her ability to manage conflict and to look at the strategies they currently use.

From these questionnaires the reader will be able to set learning objectives for the book, and on finishing the text, see how much he or she has been able to relate to the very personal world of self.

The main body of the text provides a theoretical background to the issues of managing conflict in the environment of the real world. The text closes with a case study, a series of exercises and a section on Application Planning.

Our firm belief is that when 'all is said and done, there is more said than done'. We are asking our readers to make a real commitment to use the material and become more effective in their chosen professions.

Introduction

If the word conflict conjures up the image of two bruisers battling it out to the death, this book may well come as a surprise.

> The Human Resource Director of a national charity asked us to work with his Executive Board. The Board consisted of six full-time directors and six lay members – the 'wise and the good'. The full time directors worked well together but when the full Board of 12 met, lay and full-time members, nothing happened. The HRM Director put it very simply – 'We are all too nice. Nobody challenges anything, we discuss minutiae and skate round any discussion of principle. The lay members were called in to challenge principles. They don't even complain if the coffee is cold. When the full meeting is over, we send them packing and breathe a sign of relief, get on with our work and hope that the next month's full Board meeting gets cancelled.'

Without constructive conflict 'nothing happens', but there are limits:

> We were called to work with the Board of a UK subsidiary of a German manufacturer. The Managing Director's problem was dysfunctional conflict – also leading to nothing getting done. During our work with him – what trainers call 'team-building exercises' – we met the conflict head on. The outsiders' impression was, in lay terms, that they hated each other. One director left immediately before our work with them and another resigned during the team-building exercise itself. Later, but not much later, another director resigned and the CEO was faced with the problem, in this case welcome, of building a new team virtually from scratch.

This book is about establishing the middle way – a situation where people are able to speak their minds, with due concern for others, and trust others to be honest with them. Managing interpersonal conflict is about maintaining the middle way and is a major management skill that will bring together many of the skills discussed in the other titles of this series.

Skill Pre-assessment

Diagnostic Surveys for Managing Conflict

Managing Interpersonal Conflict

Instructions

Step 1: Before you read the material in this book, please respond to the following statements by writing a number from the rating scale below in the left-hand column (Pre-assessment). Your answers should reflect your attitudes and behaviour as they are now, not as you would like them to be. Be honest. This instrument is designed to help you discover your level of competence in managing conflict so that you can tailor your learning to your specific needs. When you have completed the survey, use the Scoring Key at the end of the book (page 89) to identify the skill areas that are most important for you to master.

Step 2: After you have completed the reading and the exercises in this book, and ideally as many as you can of the Skill Application assignments at the end of this book, cover up your first set of answers. Then respond to the same statements again, this time in the right-hand column (Post-assessment). When you have completed the survey, use the Scoring Key at the end of the book (page 89) to measure your progress. If your score remains low in specific skill areas, use the behavioural guidelines at the end of the Skill Learning section (page 53) to guide further practice.

Rating Scale

6   Strongly agree   5   Agree   4   Slightly agree
3   Slightly disagree   2   Disagree   1   Strongly disagree

ASSESSMENT

PRE-	POST-	
		On a personal level when I am working with others, and I feel that things are not going as they should be and I need to take a hand,

_____ _____   1. I avoid making personal accusations and attributing self-serving motives to the other person.

_____ _____   2. When stating my concerns, I present them as my problems.

_____ _____   3. I describe the problem concisely in terms of the behaviour that occurred, its consequences and my feelings about it.

_____ _____   4. I specify the expectations and the standards that have been violated.

_____ _____   5. I make a specific request, detailing a more acceptable option.

_____ _____   6. I stay with my point of view until it is understood by the others.

_____ _____   7. I encourage a dialogue by getting others to discuss their perspectives.

_____ _____   8. When there are several concerns, I approach the issues one at a time, starting with the most straight forward and progressing to the more complex.

When someone complains about something I've done,

_____ _____   9. I look for our common areas of agreement.

_____ _____ 10. I show genuine concern and interest, even when I disagree.

_____ _____ 11. I avoid justifying my actions and become defensive.

_____ _____ 12. I seek additional information by asking questions that provide specific and descriptive information.

_____ _____ 13. I focus on one issue at a time.

_____ _____ 14. I find some aspects of the complaint with which I can agree.

_____ _____ 15. I ask the other person to suggest more acceptable behaviours.

_____ _____ 16. I strive to reach agreement on a remedial plan of action.

When I find myself in the position of a mediator between two other people in dysfunctional conflict,

_____ _____ 17. I acknowledge that conflict exists and treat it as serious and important.

_____ _____ 18. I help create an agenda for the problem-solving meeting by identifying the issues to be discussed one at a time.

_____ _____ 19. I do not take sides but remain neutral.

_____ _____ 20. I help focus the discussion on the impact of the conflict on work performance.
_____ _____ 21. I keep the interaction focused on problems rather than on personalities.
_____ _____ 22. I make certain that neither party dominates the conversation.
_____ _____ 23. I help the parties generate multiple alternatives.
_____ _____ 24. I help the parties find areas on which they agree.

Strategies for Handling Conflict

Instructions

Indicate how often you use each of the following by circling the appropriate number. After you have completed the survey, use the Scoring Key at the end of the book (page 90) to tabulate your results. Information on these five strategies is shown in Table 4 in the Skill Learning section (page 27).

Actions	Rarely				Always
1. I will stick with my position whatever.	1	2	3	4	5
2. I try to put the needs of others above mine.	1	2	3	4	5
3. I try to arrive at a compromise both parties can accept.	1	2	3	4	5
4. I try not to get involved in conflicts.	1	2	3	4	5
5. I strive to investigate issues, jointly and properly.	1	2	3	4	5
6. I try to find fault in the other person's position.	1	2	3	4	5
7. I strive to foster harmony.	1	2	3	4	5
8. I negotiate to get a portion of what I propose.	1	2	3	4	5
9. I avoid open discussions of controversial subjects.	1	2	3	4	5
10. I share information openly with others in resolving disagreements.	1	2	3	4	5
11. I enjoy winning an argument.	1	2	3	4	5
12. I go along with the suggestions of others.	1	2	3	4	5
13. I look for a middle ground to resolve disagreements.	1	2	3	4	5
14. I keep my true feelings to myself to avoid hard feelings.	1	2	3	4	5
15. I encourage the open sharing of concerns and issues.	1	2	3	4	5
16. I am reluctant to admit I am wrong.	1	2	3	4	5
17. I try to help others avoid losing face in a disagreement.	1	2	3	4	5
18. I stress the advantages of give and take.	1	2	3	4	5
19. I encourage others to take the lead in resolving controversy.	1	2	3	4	5
20. I state my position as only one point of view.	1	2	3	4	5

Skill Learning

The Management Conflict

Between one-half and two-thirds of company mergers fail. Why? One major reason is that key executives in the merging firms can't agree on their respective roles, status and 'perks'. The tensions are compounded by disagreements over which procedures to use and whose 'corporate culture' will dominate. The inability or willingness to resolve these conflicts can unravel an otherwise attractive business marriage.

Source: abstracted from 'Do Mergers Really Work?' *Business Week*, 3 June, 1985, pp. 88–100.

Paradoxically one of the leading causes of business failure among major companies is too much agreement among top management. They have similar training and experience, and this leads them to view conditions in the same way and to pursue similar goals. This problem is compounded by Boards of Directors failing to play an aggressive overview role. They avoid conflict with the internal management team who appear unified on key issues and very confident of their positions.

Source: abstracted from J. Argenti. Corporate Collapse: The Causes and Symptoms. New York: Wiley, 1976.

Mr Bernd Pischetsrieder, chairman of the BMW management board, is to meet Mr Nobuhiko Kawamoto, chief executive of Honda in Tokyo next week in a first round of talks aimed at maintaining the alliance between the Japanese car-maker and Rover.

BMW stunned Honda on Monday with its £800m take-over from British Aerospace of an 80 per cent stake in the UK car-maker. Honda still holds the remaining 20 per cent of the equity in Rover and Land Rover vehicle operations.

Mr Pischetsrieder is anxious to maintain Honda as a partner for Rover in vehicle production and development, at least in the medium term.

Honda and Rover have forged a close relationship in the past 14 years, and Mr Kawamoto was quick to express dismay at the entry of

BMW as the majority owner of Rover. He said that the BMW take-over 'negated' the long-term efforts of Honda and Rover to establish a firm future for Rover as 'a British company with its own brand identity'.

Honda's resentment at the way that British Aerospace engineered the BMW take-over of Rover was also highlighted when Mr Andrew Jones, the company's UK plant manager, admitted the company was shocked by the deal.

Source: *Financial Times*, 2 February, 1994.

Interpersonal conflict correctly used, is an essential, ubiquitous part of organisational life. Organisations in which there is little disagreement generally fail in competitive environments. Members are either so homogeneous that they are ill-equipped to adapt to change, or so complacent that they see no need to change or improve. Conflict is the life-blood of vibrant, progressive, stimulating organisations. It sparks creativity, stimulates innovation and encourages personal improvement (Robbins, 1978; King, 1981; Thomas, 1977; Wanous and Youtz, 1986).

This view is clearly in line with the management philosophy of Andrew Grove, President of INTEL.

'Many managers seem to think it is impossible to tackle anything or anyone head-on, even in business. By contrast, we at INTEL believe that it is the essence of corporate health to bring a problem out into the open as soon as possible, even if this entails a confrontation. Dealing with conflicts lies at the heart of managing any business. As a result, confrontation of issues about which there is disagreement, can be avoided only at the manager's peril. Workplace politicking grows quietly in the dark, like mushrooms; neither can stand the light of day'.

Source: *Fortune*, 23 July, 1984, p.74

Our quotes show both sides of conflict – beneficial and dysfunctional. Some people have a very low tolerance for disagreement. Whether this is the result of family background, cultural values or personality characteristics, a high level of interpersonal conflict saps their energy and demoralises their spirit. Also, some types of conflicts, regardless of frequency, generally produce dysfunctional outcomes. Examples of these would include conflicts stimulated for self-serving ends and petty personality conflicts, and arguments over things that can't be changed. Some managers, for example, feel so unsure of their qualifications and support that they continually stir up conflicts between subordinates. Out of personal inadequacy they subscribe to the 'divide and rule' philosophy.

While most writers would agree that some conflict is both inevitable and necessary in effective organisations, a well-known psychologist, Abraham Maslow (1965), has observed a high degree of ambivalence regarding the value of conflict. Maslow notes that managers intellectually appreciate the value of conflict and competition. They agree it is a necessary ingredient of the free-enterprise system. However, their actions demonstrate a personal preference for avoiding conflicts whenever possible. Belbin (1981) emphasises the importance in teams of both balance and constructive conflict.

> In Belbin's early work he constructed teams from managers attending a training programme on the basis of their IQs, and got the teams to perform competitive exercises. The teams with the highest IQs performed irregularly both from the point of view of conflict and results. The lowest IQ teams performed dully – little conflict and mediocre results. The addition or planting of a 'sparky' individual to the dull group caused both conflict and a considerable improvement in performance.

This tension between intellectual acceptance of a principle and emotional rejection of its enactment was more systematically studied in Boulding's classic study of decision-making (Boulding, 1964).

> Several groups of managers were formed to solve a complex problem. They were told their performance would be judged by a panel of experts in terms of the quantity and quality of solutions generated. The groups were identical in size and composition, with the exception that half of them included a 'mole'. Before the experiment began, the researcher instructed this person to play the role of 'devil's advocate'. This person was to challenge the group's conclusions, forcing the others to examine critically their assumptions and the logic of their arguments. At the end of the problem-solving period, the

recommendations made by both sets of groups were compared. The groups with the devil's advocates had performed significantly better on the task. They had generated more alternatives and their proposals were judged as superior. After a short break, the groups were reassembled and told that they would be performing a similar task during the next session. However, before they began discussing the next problem, they were given permission to eliminate one member. In every group containing a 'mole', he or she was the one asked to leave. The fact that every high-performance group expelled their unique competitive advantage because that member made others feel uncomfortable demonstrates a widely-shared reaction to conflict: 'I know it has positive outcomes for the performance of the organisation as a whole, but I don't like how it makes me feel personally'.

We believe that much of the ambivalence toward conflict stems from a lack of understanding of the causes of conflict, the variety of modes for managing it effectively and from a lack of confidence in one's personal skills for handling the tense, emotionally-charged environment typical of most interpersonal confrontations. It is natural for an untrained or inexperienced person to avoid threatening situations, and it is generally acknowledged that conflict represents the most severe test of a manager's interpersonal skills. The task of the effective manager, therefore, is to maintain an optimal level of conflict, while keeping conflicts focused on productive purposes (Robbins, 1974; Kelly, 1970; Thomas, 1976).

The balance requires two sets of skills. Managers must be able to:

- Diagnose the causes of conflict and select the appropriate conflict management technique
- Settle interpersonal disputes in such a way that the underlying problems are resolved and the interpersonal relationship between the disputants is not damaged

These two broad skills will be discussed in turn.

Diagnosing the Sources of Interpersonal Confrontations

Managers often behave as though serious interpersonal confrontations are the result of personality defects. They label people who are frequently involved in conflicts as 'troublemakers' or apples', and attempt to transfer or dismiss them. While some individuals seem to have a propensity for making trouble and appear to be cantankerous under even the best of circumstances, 'sour dispositions' actually account for only a small percentage of organisational conflicts (Schmidt and Tannenbaum, 1965; Hines, 1980).

This proposition is supported by research on performance appraisals (Latham and Wexley, 1981). It has been shown that managers generally attribute poor performance to personal deficiencies in workers (e.g., laziness, lack of skill, lack of motivation). However, when workers are asked the causes of their poor performance, they generally explain it in terms of problems in their environment (e.g., insufficient supplies, uncooperative co-workers). While some face-saving is obviously involved here, the line of research suggests that managers need to guard against the reflexive tendency to assume that bad behaviours imply bad people. In fact, the aggressive or harsh behaviours sometimes observed in interpersonal confrontations often reflect the frustrations of people who have good intentions but are unskilled in handling intense, emotional experiences.

In contrast to the personality-defect theory of conflict, we propose four explanations for interpersonal conflict in Table 1. These are personal differences, information deficiency, role incompatibility and environmental stress.

Table 1   Sources of conflict

Sources of conflict	Focus of conflict
Personal differences	Perceptions and expectations
Information deficiency	Misinformation and misrepresentation
Role incompatibility	Goals and responsibilities
Environmental stress	Resource scarcity and uncertainty

Personal Differences

Individuals bring different attitudes to their roles in organisations. Their values and needs have been shaped by different socialisation processes, depending on their cultural and family traditions, level of education, breadth of experience, etc. As a result, their interpretations of events and their expectations about relationships with others in the organisation will vary considerably. Conflicts stemming from incompatible personal values and needs are some of the most difficult to resolve. They often become highly emotional and take on moral overtones. A disagreement about who is factually correct easily turns into a bitter argument over who is morally *right*.

> For example, the following situation occurred in a major American company between a 63-year-old white executive vice-president and a 35-year-old black member of the corporate legal department who had been very active in the civil-rights movement during the 1960s. They disagreed vehemently over whether the company should accept a very attractive offer from the South African government to build a manufacturing facility. The vice-president felt the company had a responsibility to its stockholders to pursue every legal opportunity to increase profits. In contrast, the lawyer felt that collaborating with the South African government was tantamount to condoning apartheid.

Information Deficiency

Conflicts can arise from deficiencies in the organisation's information system. An important message may not be received, a boss's instructions may be misinterpreted, or decision-makers may arrive at different conclusions because they used different data bases. Conflicts based on misinformation or misunderstanding tend to be factual, in the sense that clarifying previous messages or obtaining additional information generally resolves the dispute. This might entail rewording the boss's instructions, reconciling contradictory sources of data, or redistributing copies of misplaced messages. This type of conflict is very common in organisations, but it is also easy to resolve. Because value systems are not being challenged, these confrontations tend to be less emotional. Once the breakdown in the information system is repaired, the disputants are generally able to resolve their disagreement with a minimum of resentment.

Role Incompatibility

The complexity inherent in most organisations tends to produce conflict between members whose tasks are interdependent, but whose roles are incompatible. This type of conflict is exemplified by the classic goal conflicts between line and staff, production and sales, marketing and research and development (R&D). Each unit has different responsibilities in the organisation and as a result, each places different priorities on organisational goals (e.g., customer satisfaction, product quality, production efficiency, compliance with European Union directives). It is also typical of firms whose multiple product lines compete for scarce resources.

> In the early days at Apple Computer, the Apple II division accounted for a large part of the company's revenue. It viewed the newly-created Macintosh division as an unwise speculative venture. The natural rivalry was made worse when a champion of Macintosh referred to the Apple II team as 'the dull and boring product division'. Since this type of conflict stems from the fundamental incompatibility of the job responsibilities of the disputants, it can often be resolved only through the mediation of a common superior.
>
> Source: summarised from *Odyssey, Pepsi to Apple*, John Sculley and John A. Bryne (1989).

Conflicts arising from role incompatibility interact with personal differences and the way individuals seek power and influence. Personal differences may well lay dormant until individuals are forced to work together with unclear organisational boundaries. Members may also perceive that their assigned roles are incompatible because they are operating from different bases of information. They communicate with different sets of people, are tied into different reporting systems and receive instructions from different bosses.

Environmentally-Induced Stress

Conflicts stemming from personal differences and role incompatibilities are greatly exacerbated by a stressful environment. For example, when an organisation is forced to operate on an austere budget, its members are more likely to become embroiled in disputes over territorial claims and resource requests. Scarcity tends to lower trust, increase awareness of sexual, racial and class differences and reduce participation in decision-making. These are ideal conditions for incubating interpersonal conflict (Cameron, Kim and Whetten, 1987).

> When a large bank announced major staff reductions, the threat to employees' security was so severe that it disrupted long-term, close working relationships. Even friendships were not immune to the effects of the stress induced by the enforced changes. Long-standing golf partnerships and car pools were disbanded because the tension among members was so high.

A second environmental condition that fosters conflict is **uncertainty**. When individuals find it difficult to predict what is going to happen to them from month to month, they become very anxious and prone to conflict. This type of 'frustration conflict' often stems from rapid, repeated change. If the way jobs are allocated, management philosophy, accounting procedures and lines of authority are changed frequently, members find it difficult to cope with the resulting stress. Sharp, bitter conflicts can easily erupt over seemingly trivial problems. This type of conflict is generally very intense, but dissipates quickly once a change becomes a routine and individuals' stress levels are lowered.

> For example, when a major pet-food manufacturer announced that one-third of its managers would have to support a new third shift, the feared disruption of personal and family routines prompted many managers to consider resigning. In addition, the uncertainty of who was going to be required to work at night was so great that even routine management work was disrupted by posturing and infighting.

The issues often come to the fore when management decides that change is needed.

> Marks and Spencer has been a paragon of the well-managed store group and in the 1980s was judged by its own management as risking smugness. They decided, as an experiment, to introduce a group of highly motivated and brilliant young graduates to 'stir things up'. The

outsiders were given a vague brief and appointed to various stores throughout the country.

A fairly typical story was of a newcomer who set up an in-store promotion to sell some slow-moving goods. He found, after he had invested a great deal of time and effort in providing point-of-sale publicity, that the whole concept was against Marks and Spencers philosophy and he had to stop it.

The newcomers went two ways – they became so completely enveloped in the M&S culture as to be barriers to change in themselves, or they left.

Conflict Response Alternatives

Now that we have examined the typical causes of conflict, we will discuss common responses. In the Pre-assessment survey, we showed that conflict falls into five categories:

- Forcing
- Accommodating
- Avoiding
- Compromising
- Collaborating

(Filley, 1975, 1978; Robbins, 1974).

Each category can be organised along two dimensions, as shown in Figure 1 (Ruble and Thomas, 1976). The five approaches to conflict reflect different degrees of cooperation and assertiveness. The cooperations dimension reflects the importance of the relationship, whereas the assertiveness dimension reflects individual's attempts to satisfy their own concerns.

The Forcing Response (assertive, uncooperative)
This is an attempt to satisfy one's own needs at the expense of the other person's. This can be done by using formal authority, physical threats, manipulation ploys or simply by ignoring the claims of the other party. The blatant use of the authority of one's office (i.e., 'I'm the boss, so we'll do it my way') or a related form of intimidation is generally evidence of a lack of tolerance or self-confidence. The use of manipulation or feigned ignorance is a

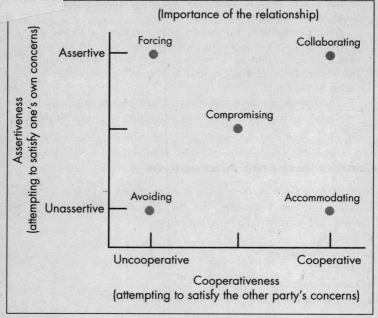

FIGURE 1   Two-dimensional model of conflict behaviour

Source: adapted from Ruble and Thomas, 1976, p 145

much more subtle reflection of egoistic leadership style. Manipulative leaders often appear to be democratic by proposing that conflicting proposals be referred to a committee for further investigation. However, they make sure that the composition of the committee reflects their interests and preferences so that what appears to be a selection based on merit is actually an authoritarian act. A related ploy used by some managers is to ignore a proposal that threatens their personal interests. If the originator inquires about the receipt of his or her memo, the manager pleads ignorance, blames the new secretary and then suggests that the proposal be redrafted. After several of these encounters, subordinates generally get the message that the boss isn't interested in their ideas.

The problem with the repeated use of the forcing approach is that it breeds hostility and resentment. While observers may intellectually admire authoritarian or manipulative leaders because they appear to accomplish a great deal, these management styles generally produce a backlash in the long run as people become unwilling to absorb the emotional cost.

The Accommodating Approach (cooperative, unassertive)
This satisfies the other party's concerns while neglecting one's own. Unfortunately, as in the case of boards of directors of failing firms who neglect their interests (and responsibilities) in favour of accommodating the wishes of management, this strategy generally results in both parties losing. The difficulty with the habitual use of the accommodating approach is that it emphasises preserving a friendly relationship at the expense of appraising issues critically and protecting personal rights. This may result in others taking advantage of you, lowering your self-esteem as you observe yourself being used by others to accomplish their objectives while you fail to make any progress toward your own.

The Avoiding Response (uncooperative, unassertive)
This neglects the interests of both parties by side-stepping the conflict or postponing a solution. The avoiding response is often the response of managers who are emotionally ill-prepared to cope with the stress associated with confrontations. It might also reflect recognition that a relationship is not strong enough to absorb the fall-out of an intense conflict. The repeated use of this approach causes considerable frustration for others because issues never seem to get resolved, tough problems are avoided because of their high potential for conflict, and the subordinates engaging in conflict are reprimanded for undermining the harmony of the work group. Sensing a leadership vacuum, people from all directions rush to fill it, creating considerable confusion and animosity in the process.

The Compromising Response
This is intermediate between assertiveness and cooperation. A compromise is an attempt to obtain partial satisfaction for both parties, in the sense that both receive the proverbial 'half a loaf'.

To accommodate this, both parties are asked to make sacrifices to obtain a common gain. While this approach has considerable practical appeal to managers, its indiscriminate use is counter-productive. If subordinates are continually told to 'split the difference', they may conclude that their managers are more inter-ested in resolving disputes than in solving problems. This creates a climate of expediency that encourages game playing, such as asking for twice as many resources as you need.

We see a common mistake in trying to appear fair to both parties by compromising on competing corporate policies and practices at all levels – strategy to redundancy. When decisions are made on the basis of 'spreading the pain evenly' or 'using half of your procedures and half of ours', rather than on the basis of merit, then harmony takes priority over value. Ironically, actions taken in the name of 'keeping peace in the merged families' often end up being so illogical and impractical that the emerging union is doomed to operate under a pall of constant internal turmoil and conflict.

Collaboration (cooperative, assertive)

This is an attempt to fully address the concerns of both parties. It is often referred to as the 'problem-solving' mode. The intent is to find solutions to the cause of the conflict that are satisfactory to both parties rather than to find fault or assign blame. In this way both parties can feel that they have 'won'. This is the only win–win strategy among the five. The avoiding mode results in a lose-lose outcome and the compromising, accommodating and forcing modes all represent win-lose outcomes. Although we will point out later that the collaboration approach is not appropriate for all situ-ations, when it is used appropriately, it has the most beneficial effect on the parties involved. It encourages norms of collabora-tion and trust while acknowledging the value of assertiveness. It encourages individuals to focus their disputes on problems and issues rather than on personalities. Finally, it cultivates the skills necessary for self-government, in the sense that effective problem-solvers feel empowered.

A comparison of the five conflict management approaches is shown in Table 2.

Table 2 A comparison of five conflict management approaches

Approach	Objective	Your posture	Supporting rationale	Likely outcome
1. Forcing	Get your way.	'I know what's right. Don't question my judgement or authority.'	It is better to risk causing a few hard feelings than to abandon the issue.	You feel vindicated, but the other party feels defeated and possibly humiliated.
2. Avoiding	Avoid having to deal with conflict.	'I'm neutral on that issue. Let me think about it. That's someone else's problem.'	Disagreements are inherently bad because they create tension.	Interpersonal problems don't get resolved, causing long-term frustration manifested in a variety of ways.
3. Compromising	Reach an agreement quickly.	'Let's search for a solution we can both live with so we can get on with our work.'	Prolonged conflicts distract people from their work and cause bitter feelings.	Participants go for the expedient, rather than effective, solutions.
4. Accommodating	Don't upset the other person.	'How can I help you feel good about this? My position isn't so important that it is worth risking bad feelings between us.'	Maintaining harmonious relationships should be our top priority.	The other person is likely to take advantage.
5. Collaborating	Solve the problem together.	'This is my position, what is yours? I'm committed to finding the best possible solution. What do the facts suggest?'	Each position is important though not necessarily equally valid. Emphasis should be placed on the quality of the outcome and the fairness of the decision-making process.	The problem is most likely to be resolved. Also, both parties are committed to the solution and satisfied that they have been treated fairly.

Negotiation Strategies

Recently, a number of academics studying organisations have noted the similarities between conflict management and negotiation strategies (Savage, Blair and Sorenson, 1989; Smith, 1987). Negotiation strategies are commonly divided into two types: **integrative** and **distributive**. Negotiators who focus on dividing up a 'fixed pie' use distributive bargaining techniques, whereas parties interested in integrative outcomes search for collaborative ways of expanding 'the pie' by avoiding fixed, incompatible positions. Distributive negotiators assume an adversarial, competitive posture. They assume that one of the parties can improve only at the other party's expense. In contrast, integrative bargainers use problem-solving techniques to find 'win-win' outcomes. They are interested in finding the best solution rather than forcing a choice between the parties' preferred solutions (Fisher and Brown, 1988; Bazerman, 1986; Pruitt, 1983).

Table 3 shows that four of the five conflict management strategies involve one or both parties sacrificing something in order to resolve the conflict. Compromising, forcing, accommodating and avoiding are **distributive solutions**. Compromise occurs when both parties make sacrifices in order to find common ground. Compromisers are generally more interested in finding an expedient solution than they are in finding an integrative solution. Forcing and accommodating demand that one party give up its position in order for the conflict to be resolved. When parties to a conflict avoid resolution, they do so because they assume that the costs of resolving the conflict are so high that they

Table 3 Comparison between negotiation and conflict-management strategies

	Distributive	Integrative
NEGOTIATION STRATEGIES		
CONFLICT MANAGEMENT STRATEGIES	Compromising Forcing Accommodating Avoiding	Collaborating

are better off not even attempting resolution. The 'fixed pie' still exists, but the individuals involved view attempts to divide it as threatening, and so they avoid decisions regarding the allocation process altogether.

Unfortunately, distributive negotiation strategies are consistent with the natural inclination of many individuals to approach conflicts from a 'macho man', 'easy-touch' or 'split-the-difference' perspective. The problem with the frequent use of these negotiation strategies is that they engender competition, exploitation or irresponsibility.

The forcing approach to negotiations, in particular, has intuitive appeal. In the eyes of many, effective negotiators are tough, highly combative and even ruthless when necessary. However, research has clearly demonstrated that this 'the end justifies the means' view of negotiation is generally ineffective and frequently counter-productive.

Later we will discuss the limited circumstances under which all forms of conflict management are appropriate. However, as a general-purpose strategy, the integrative approach is far superior. When adopted as an organising framework, the following integrative negotiation strategies have been shown to foster collaboration (Northcraft and Neale, 1990).

1. **Establish common goals.** To begin with, in order to foster a climate of collaboration, both parties need to focus on what they have in common. Focusing on their shared goals – e.g. increased productivity, lower costs, reduced design time or improved relations between departments – sensitises the parties to the merits of resolving their differences in a way that avoids jeopardising their mutual goals. The step is characterised by the general question, 'What common goals provide a context for these discussions?'

2. **Separate the people from the problem.** Having clarified the mutual benefits to be gained by successfully concluding a negotiation, it is useful to focus attention on the real issue at hand and solve the actual problem. As noted in the book – *Effective Communication*, negotiations are more likely to result in mutual satisfaction if the parties depersonalise the discussions.

Integrative negotiators suppress their personal feelings and the other party is viewed as the advocate of a point of view, rather than as a rival. The integrative bargainer would say, 'That is an unreasonable position' rather than 'You are an unreasonable person'.

3. **Focus on interests, not positions.** Positions are demands the negotiator makes. Interests are the reasons behind the demands. Experience shows that it is easier to establish agreement on interests, given that they tend to be broader and multi-faceted. Recalling the discussion on creative problem-solving in the book *Effective Problem-Solving*, this step involves redefining and broadening the problem to make it more tractable. That book contains several techniques for facilitating this process. When a variety of issues are examined, parties are better able to understand each other's point of view and place their own views in perspective. The integrative question is 'Help me understand why you are advocating that position?'

4. **Invent options for mutual gains.** This step also involves creativity, although this time it is focused on generating unusual solutions. Although it is true that some negotiations may necessarily be distributive, it is a mistake for negotiators to automatically adopt a win-lose posture. By focusing both parties' attention on the brainstorming alternatives to find mutually agreeable solutions, the negotiation dynamics naturally shift from competitive to collaborative. In addition, the more options and combinations there are to explore, the greater the probability of reaching an integrative solution. The integrative negotiator offers, 'Now that we better understand each others' underlying concerns and objectives, let's brainstorm ways of satisfying the needs of us both.'

5. **Use objective criteria.** No matter how integrative both parties might be, there are bound to be some incompatible interests. Rather than seizing on these as opportunities for testing wills, it is far more productive to determine what is fair. This requires both parties to examine how fairness should be judged. This shift in thinking from 'getting what I want' to

deciding 'what makes most sense' fosters an open, reasonable attitude. It encourages parties to avoid over-confidence or over-commitment to their initial position. This approach is characterised by asking, 'What is a fair way to evaluate the merits of our arguments?'

6. **Define success in terms of gains, not losses.** If a manager seeks a ten per cent salary rise and receives only six per cent, that outcome can be viewed as either a six per cent improvement or as a 40 per cent shortfall. The first interpretation focuses on gains, the second on losses – in this case, unrealised expectations. The outcome is the same, but the manager's satisfaction with it varies substantially. It is important to recognise that our satisfaction with an outcome is affected by the standards we use to judge it. Recognising this, the integrative negotiator sets reasonable standards by which to judge the value of proposed solutions. The integrative approach to assessing proposals is, 'Does this outcome constitute a meaningful improvement in current conditions?'

What happens if you are trying to collaborate and the other party is using combative, high-pressure negotiation tactics? Should you simply persist, hoping the other party will eventually follow suit, while at the same time risking the other party taking advantage of your non-combative posture? Or should you risk the possibility that you will eventually become so frustrated that you'll join the fracas?

In essence, the guidelines suggest shifting the focus of the discussion from 'content' to 'process'. By presenting your frustration, you are able to draw attention to the unsatisfactory negotiation process. In the course of a conversation of this type, the other party's underlying reasons for using a particular negotiation style often surface, and this information about time pressure, or lack of trust, or unrealistic expectations can be used to build a more collaborative mode of interaction – 'How can we work together to resolve our concerns about process so that they don't impair the outcome of our discussion?'

Selecting the Appropriate Approach

The comparison of alternative approaches inevitably leads to the question, 'Which one is best?' While the collaborative approach produces the fewest negative side effects, all the approaches have their place. The appropriateness of a management strategy depends on its congruence with both personal style and situational demands.

The five modes of handling conflict are not equally attractive to all individuals. Each of us tends to have a preferred strategy that is consistent with the value we place on conflict and with our **dominant personality characteristics** (Cummings, Harnett and Stevens, 1971; Porter, 1973). The research has identified three distinct personality profiles:

- The **altruistic-nurturing** personality seeks gratification through promoting harmony with others and enhancing their welfare, with little concern for being rewarded in return. This personality type is characterised by trust, optimism, idealism and loyalty.
- The **assertive-directing** personality seeks gratification through self-assertion and directing the activities of others with a clear sense of having earned rewards. Individuals with this personality characteristic tend to be self-confident, enterprising and persuasive.
- The **analytic-autonomising** personality seeks gratification through the achievement of self-sufficiency, self-reliance and logical orderliness. This personality type is cautious, practical, methodical and principled.

When altruistic-nurturing individuals encounter conflict, they tend to press for harmony by accommodating the demands of the other party. In contrast, the assertive-directing personality tends to challenge the opposition by using the forcing approach. The analysing-autonomising personality becomes very cautious when encountering conflict. Initially an attempt is made to rationally resolve the problem. However, if the conflict becomes very intense, this individual will withdraw and break contact.

While there appears to be a strong link between dominant

personality characteristics and preferred modes of handling conflict, research on leadership styles has demonstrated that the most effective managers use a variety of styles (Schriesheim and Von Glinow, 1977), tailoring their response to the demands of the situation. This general principle has been borne out in research on conflict-management.

In one study, 25 executives were asked to describe two conflict situations – one with bad results and one with good (Phillips and Cheston, 1979). These incidents were then categorised in terms of the conflict-management approach used. As shown in Figure 2 (next page), there were 23 incidents of forcing, 12 incidents of problem-solving, five incidents of compromise and 12 incidents of avoidance. Admittedly, this was a very small sample of managers, but the fact that there were almost twice as many incidents of forcing as problem-solving and nearly five times as many as compromising is noteworthy. It is also interesting that the executives indicated that forcing and compromising were equally as likely to produce good as bad results, whereas problem-solving was always linked with positive outcomes, and avoidance generally led to negative results.

It is striking that, despite the fact that forcing was as likely to produce bad as good results, it was by far the most commonly used conflict-management mode. Since this approach is clearly not superior in terms of results, one wonders why these senior executives reported a propensity for using it.

A likely answer is expediency. Evidence for this supposition is provided by a study of the preferred influence strategies of over 300 managers in three countries (Kipnis and Schmidt, 1983).

The study reports that when subordinates refuse or appear reluctant to comply with a request, managers become directive. When resistance in subordinates is encountered, managers tend to fall back on their superior power and insist on compliance. So pervasive was this pattern that Kipnis and Schmidt proposed an 'Iron Law of Power': 'The greater discrepancy in power between influence and target, the greater the probability that more directive influence strategies will be used'.

A second striking feature of Figure 2 is that some conflict-

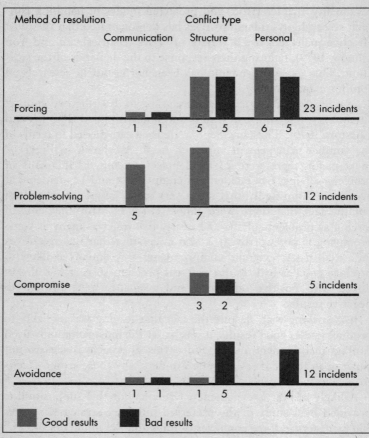

FIGURE 2 Outcome of conflict – resolution by conflict type and method of resolution.

Source: Phillips and Cheston 1979.

management approaches were never used for certain types of issues. In particular, the managers did not report a single case of problem-solving or compromising when personal problems were the source of the conflict. These approaches were used primarily for managing conflicts involving incompatible goals and conflicting reward systems between departments. Two conclusions can be drawn from this study. First, no one approach is most effective for managing every type of conflict. Second, managers are more effective in dealing with conflicts if they feel comfortable using a variety of approaches. These conclusions point out the need to understand the conditions under which each conflict-management technique is most effective. This knowledge allows one to match the characteristics of a conflict incident with the management techniques best suited to those characteristics. The situational factors that should be considered are summarised in Table 4.

Table 4 Matching the conflict management approach with the situation

| Situational considerations | Conflict-management approach | | | | |
	Forcing	Accommo-dating	Compro-mising	Collabo-rating	Avoiding
Issue importance	High	Low	Med	High	Low
Relationship importance	Low	High	Med	High	Low
Relative power	High	Low	Equal-High	Low-High	Equal-High
Time constraints	Med-High	Med-High	Low	Low	Med-High

The **forcing** approach is most appropriate when a conflict of values or perspectives is involved and one feels compelled to defend the 'correct' position; when a superior–subordinate relationship is involved; when maintaining a close, supportive relationship is not critical; and when there is a sense of urgency. An example of such a situation might be a manager's insisting that a new recruit follow important company safety regulations.

The **accommodating** approach is most appropriate when the importance of maintaining a good working relationship outweighs all other considerations. While this could be the case regardless of your formal relationship with the other party, it is often perceived as being the only option for subordinates of powerful bosses. The nature of the issues and the amount of time available play a secondary role in determining the choice of this strategy. Accommodation becomes especially appropriate when the issues are not vital to your interests and the problem must be resolved quickly.

Trying to reach a **compromise** is most appropriate when the issues are very complex and moderately important (there are no simple solutions), and both parties have a strong interest in different facets of the problem. The other essential situational requirement is adequate time for negotiation. The classic case is a bargaining session between representatives of management and labour to avert a scheduled strike. While the characteristics of the relationship between the parties are not essential factors, experience has shown that negotiations tend to work best between parties with equal power who are committed to maintaining a good long-term relationship.

The **collaborating** approach is most appropriate when the issues are critical, maintaining an ongoing supportive relationship between peers is important, and time constraints are not pressing. Although collaboration can also be an effective approach for resolving conflicts between a superior and subordinate it is important to point out that when a conflict involves peers, the collaborative mode is more appropriate than either the forcing or accommodating approaches.

The **avoidance** approach is most appropriate when one's stake in an issue is not high and there is not a strong interpersonal reason for getting involved, regardless of whether the conflict involves a superior, subordinate or peer. A severe time constraint becomes a contributing factor because it increases the likelihood of using avoidance, by default. While one might prefer other strategies, such as compromise and collaboration, that have a good chance of resolving problems without damaging relationships, these are ruled out because of time pressure.

Resolving Interpersonal Confrontations Using the Collaborative Approach

From the discussion so far, you can see that part of the skill of effective conflict management is choosing an appropriate approach based on a thoughtful assessment of the situation. Characteristics of unsuccessful conflict-managers are their habitual reliance on one or two strategies regardless of changing circumstances, and the inability to effectively implement the collaborative approach.

In the study by Kipnis and Schmidt (1983) discussed earlier, most managers expressed general support for the collaborative approach, but when it appeared things weren't going their way, they reverted back to a directive approach.

One important reason for this pattern is that the collaborative approach to conflict management is the most difficult to implement successfully, requiring much more skill than the other systems. It is for example, a fairly simple matter for managers to either give in or impose their will, but resolving differences in a truly collaborative manner is a very complicated and taxing process. As a result, when situational conditions indicate that the collaborative approach is most appropriate, unskilled managers will often opt for less challenging approaches. To help you gain proficiency in using the collaborative approach, the remainder of this book describes behavioural guidelines for effectively resolving interpersonal confrontations.

The following guidelines for collaborative conflict management draw upon the negotiation literature discussed earlier. However, although general negotiation strategies and conflict-management approaches are similar in concept, specific negotiation tactics and conflict management guidelines tend to diverge. This is because the nature of the issues is generally different. Although there is obviously some overlap in content, negotiations tend to focus on substantive issues (e.g., responsibility for the distribution of a new product), whereas interpersonal conflicts are more likely to be triggered by an emotional confrontation (e.g., a sexual-harassment complaint). Because interpersonal confrontations involving complaints and criticisms have been shown to be the most difficult to manage in a collaborative manner, they are the focus of this section.

To facilitate the presentation of a step-by-step approach to resolving conflict by collaboration, we will treat conflict management as a problem-solving process containing four phases:

1. Problem identification
2. Solution generation
3. Action plan formulation and agreement
4. Implementation and follow-up.

In the midst of a heated discussion, problem identification and alternative generation are the most critical steps, as well as the most difficult to effectively manage. They are also the only controllable elements. That is, if you initiate a complaint, you can control how you state it and whether you request a change in behaviour. However, you cannot control whether the other party agrees to change or, having agreed, actually undertakes a follow-up. We will therefore, focus primarily on phases one and two during our skill training. Also, because during the early phases of a confrontation the participants' orientations are very different, we shall examine the role of each participant separately.

Virtually every confrontation involves two principle participants who we shall term the initiator and the responder – the one with the issue and the person required to handle it. For example, a subordinate might complain about not being given a fair share of the opportunities to work overtime (the initiator); or the head of production (the initiator) might complain to the head of sales (the responder) about frequent changes in order specifications.

Such a confrontation represents a greater challenge for responders because they basically have responsibility for transforming a complaint into a problem-solving discussion. The transformation requires considerable patience and self-confidence, particularly when the initiator is unskilled. In such circumstances the unskilled initiator will generally begin the discussion by blaming the responder for the problem and should the responder also be unskilled, he or she will adopt a defensive position and probably look for an opportunity to come back aggressively.

If these lose-lose dynamics persist, a third part, whom we shall term the mediator, is needed to cool down the initiator and the responder – to re-establish constructive communication and help the parties reconcile their differences. The presence of a mediator takes some of the pressure off the responder because an impartial referee provides assistance in moving the confrontation through the problem-solving phases.

The following guidelines provide a model for acting out the initiator, responder and mediator roles in such a way that problem-solving can occur. In our discussion of each role, we will assume that the other participants in the conflict are not behaving according to their prescribed guidelines.

The First Party – Initiator

Maintain personal ownership of the problem

It is important to recognise that when you are upset and frustrated, this is your problem, not the other person's. You may feel that your boss or co-worker is the source of your problem and resolving your frustration is your immediate concern. The first step in addressing this concern is acknowledging accountability for your feelings. Suppose someone enters your office with a smelly cigar without asking if it is all right to smoke. The fact that your office is going to stink for the rest of the day may infuriate you, but the odour does not present a problem for your smoking guest. One way to determine ownership of a problem is to identify whose needs are not being met. In this case, your need for a clean working environment is not being met, so the smelly office is your problem. Own your problems and, should it be wise to do so, explain your problem to the smoker. If the smoker happens to be your senior and is well known for his or her inability to take the mildest criticism, then we may decide that tolerating a smelly office and holding ones peace is the wisest action. Always remember the old riddle: 'What do you call a mad terrorist with a gun?' 'Sir.'

The advantage of acknowledging ownership of a problem when registering a complaint is that it reduces defensiveness (Adler, 1977). In order for you to get a problem solved, the respondent must not feel threatened by your initial statement of the problem. By beginning the conversation with a request that the responder help solve your problem, you immediately establish a problem-solving atmosphere. For example, you might say, 'Mary, have you a few minutes. I have a problem I need to discuss with you.'

Succinctly describe your problem in terms of behaviours, consequences and feelings

The key is to reduce your concern to a few words, describing what has happened, the consequences and your feelings. A useful model for remembering how to state your problem effectively has been prescribed by Gordon (1961): 'I have a problem. When you do X, Y results, and I feel Z'. While we don't advocate the memorisation of set formulas for improving communication skills, keeping the structure in mind will help you implement three critical guidelines, as follows:

1. Describe the specific **behaviours** (X) that present a problem for you. This will help you avoid what may be an automatic response to your feeling upset – giving feedback that is evaluative and general. 'Your behaviour is bad,' is a form of feedback that helps no one – specify the expectations or standards that have been violated and the recipient has an opportunity to take action, other than being defensive. For example, a subordinate may have missed a deadline for completing the job required; your boss may gradually be taking over tasks previously delegated to you; or a colleague in the accounting department may have repeatedly failed to provide you with data required for an important presentation. Say 'I am very concerned that the deadline has been missed' – be specific and detail the issue.

2. Outline the specific, **observable consequences** (Y) of these behaviours. Simply telling others that their actions are causing you problems is often sufficient stimulus for change. In fast-paced work environments, people generally become insensitive to the impact of their actions. They don't intend to cause offence but become so busy meeting deadlines associated with 'getting the product out the door' that they don't notice subtle negative feedback from others. When this occurs, bringing to

the attention of others the consequences of their behaviours will often prompt them to change.

Unfortunately, sometimes problems can't be resolved this simply. At times offenders are aware of the negative consequences of their behaviours and yet persist in them. In such cases, this approach is still useful in stimulating a rational discussion because it is non–threatening. Possibly the responders' behaviours are constrained by the expectations of their boss or by the fact that the department is currently understaffed. Responders may not be able to change these constraints, but this approach will encourage them to discuss them with you so that you can work on the problem together.

3. Describe the **feelings** (Z) you experience as a result of the problem. It is important that the responder understands that his or her behaviour is not just inconvenient but is important to YOU. You need to explain how it is affecting you personally by engendering feelings of frustration, anger and insecurity. Explain how these feelings are interfering with what you see as your job. The named behaviour is – making it more difficult for you to concentrate, to be satisfy customer demands, to be supportive of your boss, to work up the 110 per cent you know is necessary.

As we mentioned earlier, you should use this three–step model as a guide rather than as a formula. The order of the components may vary and you should not use the same words every time. For example, it would get pretty monotonous if everyone in a work group initiated a discussion about an interpersonal issue with the words 'I have a problem'. Observe how the key elements in the model are used in different ways in the following examples from Adler (1977):

> 'I have to tell you that I get upset [feelings] when you make jokes about my bad memory in front of other people [behaviour]. In fact, I get so angry that I find myself bringing up your faults to get even [consequences].'
>
> 'I have a problem. When you say you'll be here for our date at six and don't show up until after seven [behaviour], the dinner gets ruined, we're late for the show we planned to see [consequences], and I

feel hurt because it seems like I'm just not that important to you [feelings].'

'The employees want to let management know that we've been having a hard time lately with the short notice you've been giving when you need us to work overtime [behaviour]. That probably explains some of the grumbling and lack of co-operation you've mentioned [consequences]. Anyhow, we wanted to make it clear that this policy has really got a lot of the workers feeling pretty resentful [feeling].'

Avoid drawing evaluative conclusions and attributing motives to the respondent

In presenting your problem, avoid the pitfalls of making accusations, drawing inferences about motivations or intentions, or attributing the responder's undesirable behaviour to personal inadequacies. Statements such as 'You are always interrupting me', 'You haven't been fair to me since the day I disagreed with you in the board meeting', and 'You never have time to listen to our problems and suggestions because you manage your time so poorly', are good at starting rows but less effective for initiating rational problem-solving.

Another key to reducing defensiveness is to delay proposing a solution until both parties agree on the nature of the problem. When you become so upset with someone's behaviour that you feel it is necessary to initiate a complaint, it is often because the person has not met the criteria you have laid down for them. For example, you might feel that your subordinate has failed to complete a project on time. Consequently, you might begin the interview by assuming that the subordinate was aware of your time scale. If he or she is not aware of that time scale and was working to another set of priorities, we will have a potentially dysfunctional conflict. Check on common ground: 'Were you aware that the whole project has to be completed by next week and that we are waiting on your parts before we complete?' Establish common ground first. If the respondent was unaware of the deadlines or the importance of his or her contribution, then you have slipped up and not them. In this case any recriminations will lead at best to defensiveness.

Besides creating defensiveness, the principal disadvantage to initiating problem-solving with a suggested remedy without establishing common ground, is that it doesn't work. Before completing the problem-articulation phase, you have immediately jumped to the solution-generation phase, based on the assumption that you know all the reasons for, and constraints on, the other person's behaviour. As discussed in the book of this series *Effective Problem-Solving*, you will jointly produce better, more acceptable solutions if you present your statement of the problem and discuss that thoroughly before beginning to discuss potential solutions.

Persist until understood

There are times when the other person will not clearly receive or acknowledge even the most effectively expressed message. Suppose, for instance, that you share the following problem with a co-worker (Adler, 1977):

> 'I've been bothered by something lately and I would like to discuss it with you. To be honest, I'm uncomfortable [feeling] when you use so much bad language [behaviour]. I don't mind an occasional 'damn' or 'hell', but the f-word is difficult for me to accept. Lately I've found myself avoiding you [consequences], and that's no good either, so I wanted to let you know how I feel.'

When you share your feelings in this non-evaluative way, it is likely that the other person will understand your position and possibly try to change behaviour to suit your needs. On the other hand, there are a number of less-satisfying responses that could be made to your comment:

> 'Listen, these days everyone talks that way. And besides, you've got your faults, too, you know!' [Your co-worker becomes defensive, rationalising and counter-attacking.]
>
> 'Yes, I suppose I do swear a lot. I'll have to work on that some day.' [Gets the general drift of your message but fails to comprehend how serious the problem is for you.]
>
> 'Listen, if you're still angry about my forgetting to tell you about that meeting the other day, you can be sure that I'm really sorry. I won't do it again.' [Totally misunderstands.]
>
> 'Speaking of avoiding, have you seen Chris lately? I wonder if anything is wrong with him.' [Is discomfited by your frustration and changes the subject.]

In each case, the co-worker does not understand or does not wish to acknowledge the problem. In these situations it is necessary to repeat your concern until it has been acknowledged as a problem to be solved. Otherwise, the problem-solving process will terminate at this point and nothing will change. Repeated assertions can take the form of either persistently restating the same phrase several times, reiterating your concern with different words or examples that you feel might improve comprehension. To avoid introducing new concerns or shifting from a descriptive to an evaluative mode, keep in mind the 'X,Y,Z' formula for feedback. Persistence is most effective when it consists of 'variations on a theme', rather than 'variation in themes'. Woods (1989) details this method as a pair of techniques – Broken Record and Fielding. Thus, he would term sticking to the core theme as using a Broken Record technique:

> Initiator – 'These goods need to be moved by tomorrow.'
> Respondent – 'There are many good reasons why these goods cannot be moved . . .'
> Initiator – 'These goods need to be moved by tomorrow.'

Such plain repetition can be seen as being effective but is hardly likely to win friends. If we wish to retain some contacts with the respondent we should advocate the use of the Fielding technique in addition to the Broken Record technique. A phrase using some of the respondents words would accompany the repetitive core theme:

> Initiator – 'The goods need to be moved by tomorrow.'
> Respondent – 'There are many good reasons why these goods cannot be moved . . .'
> Initiator – 'I fully accept that you may have good reasons (Fielding) but the goods still have to be moved by tomorrow (back to Broken Record).'

The process continues until heard by the respondent.

Encourage two-way discussion

It is important that you establish a climate for rational problem-solving by inviting the other person to express opinions and ask questions. Often there is a very simple explanation for another's behaviour, perhaps a radically different view of the problem. The sooner this information is introduced into the conversation, the sooner the issue is likely to be resolved. As a rule of thumb, the longer the opening statement of the initiator, the longer it will take the two parties to work through their problem. The reason for this is that the more lengthy the statement of the problem, the more likely it is to encourage a defensive reaction. The longer we talk, the more worked-up we get, and the more likely we are to violate the principles of supportive communication. As a result, the other party begins to feel threatened, starts mentally outlining a rebuttal or counter-attack and stops listening empathetically to our concerns. Once these dynamics enter the discussion, the collaborative approach is usually discarded in favour of the accommodation or forcing strategies, depending on the circumstances.

When this occurs, it is unlikely that the actors will be able to reach a mutually satisfactory solution to their problem without third-party intervention. Keep it simple and keep it short. Only make one point and make sure that it is the best point. Here again we return to negotiation strategy – do not produce a range of arguments, the responder will simply dispose of the weakest and ignore the strongest. **Only** play your best argument and stick to it.

Manage the agenda: approach multiple or complex problems incrementally

One way to cut down on the length of your opening statement is to approach complex problems incrementally. Rather than raising a series of issues all at once, initially focus on a fairly simple or rudimentary problem. Then, as you gain a greater appreciation for the other party's perspective and share some problem-solving success, you can proceed to discuss more challenging issues. This is especially important when you are trying to resolve a problem with a person who is important to your work performance but does not have a long-standing relationship with you. The less familiar you are with the other's opinions and personality, as well as the situational constraints influencing his or her behaviours, the more you should approach the problem-solving discussion as a fact-finding and rapport-building mission. This is best done by focusing your introductory statement on a specific manifestation of a broader problem and presenting it in such a way that it encourages the other party to respond expansively. You can then use this early feedback to shape the remainder of your agenda. For example: 'Bill, we had difficulty getting that work order processed on time yesterday. What seemed to be the problem?'

Focus on commonalties as the basis for requesting a change

Once the problem is clearly understood, the discussion should shift to the solution-generation phase of the problem-solving process. Most of us share some goals (personal and organisational), believe in many of the same fundamental principles of management, and operate under similar constraints. The most straightforward approach to changing another's offensive behaviour is making a request. The legitimacy of a request will be enhanced if it is linked to common interests. These might include shared values such as treating co-workers fairly and following through on commitments, or shared constraints such as getting reports in on time and operating within budgetary restrictions. This approach is particularly effective when the parties have had difficulty getting along in the past. In these situations, pointing out how a change in the respondent's behaviour would positively affect your shared fate will reduce her defensiveness:

> 'Jane, one of the things we have all worked hard to build in this audit team is mutual support. We are all pushed to the limit getting this job completed by the third-quarter deadline next week, and the rest of the team members find it difficult to accept your unwillingness to work overtime during this emergency. Because the allocation of next quarter's projects will be affected by our current performance, would you please decide what you intend to do.'

The Second Party or 'The Accused'

Now we shall examine the problem-identification phase from the viewpoint of the person who is supposedly the source of the problem. In a work setting, this could be a manager who is making unrealistic demands, a new employee who has ignored safety regulations or a co-worker who is claiming credit for your ideas. The overall strategy is to listen before responding. The tactics for doing this are shown in the following guidelines.

Establish a climate for joint problem-solving by showing genuine interest and concern

When a person complains to you, you should not treat that complaint lightly. While this sounds self-evident, it is often difficult to focus your attention on someone else's problems when you are in the middle of writing an important project report or concerned about preparing for a meeting scheduled to begin in a few minutes. Also, it is often wise to come prepared for a difficult meeting and preparation may well necessitate you buying time. Therefore, unless the other person's emotional condition means that you need to take immediate action, it is usually fine to agree a time for another meeting after you have understood the issue to be discussed.

In most cases, the initiator will be expecting you to set the tone for the meeting. The tones to be avoided are over-reaction or defensiveness. Even if you disagree with the complaint and feel it has no foundation, you need to respond empathetically to the initiator's statement of the problem. The initiator MAY not have expressed the criticism correctly.

> Most of us have had experience in not satisfying our bosses in the presentation of a written report. What frequently happens is that when we present a report, the grammar and even the spelling are criticised, but we would be unwise to leave it there. In experience many people find it easier to criticise the detail rather than explain their real complaint – that the report is inadequate in a much more radical way. It is the job of the respondent to tease out the 'real' criticism without dismissing the detailed complaints.

Learning from criticism is best done by conveying an attitude of interest and receptivity through your posture, tone of voice and facial expressions. One of the most difficult aspects of establishing the proper climate for your discussion is responding appropriately to the emotions of the initiator. Sometimes you may need to let a person blow off steam before trying to address the substance of a specific complaint. In some cases the therapeutic effect of being able to express negative emotions to the boss will be enough to satisfy a subordinate. This occurs frequently in high-pressure jobs where tempers flare easily as a result of the intense stress.

However, an emotional outburst can be very detrimental to problem-solving. If an employee begins verbally attacking you or someone else, and it is apparent that the individual is more interested in getting even than in solving an interpersonal problem, you may need to interrupt and interject some ground rules for collaborative problem-solving. By explaining calmly to the other person that you are willing to discuss a genuine problem but that you will not tolerate personal attacks or 'scape-goating', you can quickly determine the true intentions of the initiator. In most instances he or she will apologise, emulate your emotional tone and begin formulating a useful statement of the problem.

Techniques developed for making the most of criticism has been described by many authors. Mike Woods (1989) calls them **appropriate assertion** and **constructive enquiry**. The principle of appropriate assertion is to take the sting and negative emotion from a criticism by assertively affirming that you either agree or disagree with the comments.

> 'You are late with the training programme.' 'That is correct, the training programme has been delayed.' And then stop.
>
> If however the programme has not been delayed: 'That is completely untrue – the training programme is on schedule.' And then stop.

The clarity and the uncompromising nature of the response disarms most people who have the intention of persecuting you. Once you have 'disarmed' the initiator you can move on to the next phase of learning from the criticism. The process of 'disarming' certainly includes removing the emotional element from the criticism.

An adage that may be of use is: 'It is no use pouring the cold water of logic onto the hot coals of emotion.'

Learning from criticism involves rational problem-solving on the parts of the initiator and the respondent.

Learning from criticism

Untrained initiators will typically present complaints that are both very general and highly evaluative. They will make generalisations from a few specific incidents about your motives and your personal strengths and weaknesses. If the two of you are going to transform a personal complaint into a joint problem, you must redirect the conversation from general and evaluative accusations to descriptions of specific behaviours.

To do this, ask for details about specific actions that are forming the basis for the evaluation. You might find it useful to phrase your questions so that they reflect the 'X,Y,Z' model described previously: 'Can you give me a specific example of my behaviour that concerns you?', 'When I did that, what were the specific consequences for your work?', 'How did you feel when that happened?' When a complaint is both serious and complex, it is especially critical for you to understand it completely. In these situations, check your level of understanding by summarising the initiator's main points and asking if your summary is correct. Mike Woods, in the jargon of assertiveness training calls this **constructive enquiry**.

Sometimes it is useful to ask for additional complaints: 'Are there any other problems in our relationship you'd like to discuss?' If the initiator is just in a griping mood, this is not a good time to probe further; you don't want to encourage this type of behaviour. But if the person is seriously concerned about improving your relationship, your discussion to this point has been helpful and you suspect that the initiator is holding back and not talking about the really serious issues, you should probe deeper. Often people begin by complaining about a minor problem to 'test the water'. If you lose your temper, the conversation finishes and the really critical issues aren't discussed. However, if you are responsive to a frank discussion about problems, the more serious issues are likely to surface.

Agree with some aspect of the complaint

Appropriate assertion involves a clear acceptance or denial of the truth of criticism, unfortunately things are seldom black and white. There is an element of truth in many harsh criticisms, but this is difficult to accept. Acceptance may well fuel the complaining behaviour, so we need a further formula. In practice, this step is probably the best test of whether the responder is committed to using the collaborative approach to conflict management rather than the avoiding, forcing or accommodating approaches. People who use the forcing mode will grit their teeth while listening to the initiator, just waiting to find a flaw they can use to launch a counter-attack. Or they will simply respond, 'I'm sorry, but that's just the way I am. You'll simply have to get used to it.' Accommodators will apologise profusely and ask for forgiveness. People who avoid conflicts will acknowledge and agree with the initiator's concerns, but only in a superficial manner because their only concern is how to quickly end the awkward conversation.

In contrast, collaborators will demonstrate their concerns for both cooperation and assertiveness by looking for points in the initiator's presentation with which they can genuinely agree. By following the supportive communication guidelines discussed in the book of the same series, *Effective Communication*, you will find that it is possible to accept the other person's viewpoint without conceding your own position. Even in the most blatantly malicious and hostile verbal assault (which may be more a reflection of the initiator's insecurity than evidence of your inadequacies), there is generally a grain of truth.

> A few years ago a junior member in a business school who was being reviewed for promotion received a very unfair appraisal from one of his senior colleagues. Since the junior member knew that the critic was going through a personal crisis, he could have dismissed this criticism as irrelevant and insignificant. However, one particular phrase, 'You are stuck on a narrow line of research', kept coming back to his mind. There was something there that couldn't be ignored. As a result of turning what was otherwise a very vindictive remark into something personally useful, he accepted the partial truth of the remark and acted accordingly, changing his career path. Furthermore, by publicly giving the senior colleague credit for the suggestion, he substantially strengthened the interpersonal relationship.

There are a number of ways you can agree with part of a message without accepting it in full (Adler, 1977). You can find an element of truth and accept it:

> I accept that I may be seen to be pursuing a narrow line of research and I thank you for bringing it to my attention. (Accepting that this person may observe my behaviour in a certain way but NOT accepting that this was my intention or indeed that the remark is true.)

We may then move on and request further information and guidance:

> As I was unaware of the potential problem, perhaps you could help me by suggesting how I could be seen to broaden my approach.

Again, do not be stuck in a formal set of words.

> 'Well, I can see how you would think that. I have known people who have deliberately shirked their responsibilities.'

Or, you can agree with the person's feelings:

> 'It is obvious that our earlier discussion greatly upset you.'

Again, in none of these cases are you agreeing with the initiator's conclusions or evaluations without conceding your position. You will be seen to be listening, attempting to understand and foster a problem-solving, rather than argumentative discussion and this in itself will assist developing a supportive environment. Generally, initiators prepare for a complaint session by mentally cataloguing all the evidence supporting their point of view. Once the discussion begins, they introduce as much evidence as necessary to make their argument convincing; that is, they keep arguing until you agree. The more evidence that is introduced, the broader the argument becomes and the more difficult it is to begin investigating solutions. Consequently, establishing a basis of agreement is the key to culminating the problem-identification phase of the problem-solving process.

Ask for suggestions of acceptable alternatives
Once you are certain that you fully understand the initiator's complaint, proceed with the next aspect of constructive enquiry – look for possible solutions with the initiator. Mutual problem-solving is

an important transition in the discussion. Attention moves from negative historical aspects to positive and future concerns. It also tells the initiator that you are concerned with his or her opinions – a key element in the joint problem-solving process. Some managers listen patiently to a subordinate's complaint, express appreciation for the feedback, say they will rectify the problem, and then close the discussion. This leaves the initiator guessing about the outcome of the meeting. Will you take the complaint seriously? Will you really change? If so, will the change resolve the problem? It is important to eliminate this ambiguity by agreeing on a plan of action. If the problem is particularly serious or complex, it is useful to write down specific agreements, including assignments and deadlines, as well as providing for a follow-up meeting to check progress.

The Mediator

Frequently it is necessary for a third party to intervene in a dispute (Walton, 1969). While this may occur for a variety of reasons, we will assume in this discussion that the mediator has been invited to help the initiator and responder resolve their differences. We will further assume that the mediator is senior and concerned with both the initiator and the respondent, though this assumption is not necessary to discuss the process.

> A hair stylist in a beauty salon complained to the manager about the way the receptionist was favouring other beauticians who had been there longer. This allegation violated the manager's policy of allocating walk-in business strictly on the basis of beautician availability. The manager investigated the complaint and discovered considerable animosity between these two employees. The stylist felt the receptionist was keeping sloppy records, while the receptionist blamed the stylist for forgetting to hand in her slip when she finished with a customer. The problems between these two appeared serious enough to the participants and broad enough in scope that the manager called both parties into her office to help them resolve their differences.

The following guidelines, intended to help mediators avoid the common pitfalls associated with this role are shown in Table 5.

Table 5 Ten ways to fail as a mediator

1. After you have listened to the argument for a short time, begin to non-verbally communicate your discomfort with the discussion (e.g., sit back, begin to fidget).
2. Take sides and communicate your agreement with **one** of the parties (e.g., through facial expressions, posture, chair position, reinforcing comments).
3. Say that you shouldn't be talking about this kind of thing at work or where others can overhear.
4. Discourage the expression of emotion. Suggest that the discussion would be better held later after both parties have cooled off.
5 Suggest that both parties are wrong. Point out the problems with both points of view.
6. Suggest part-way through the discussion that possibly you aren't the person who should be helping solve this problem.
7. See if you can get both parties to attack you.
8. Minimise the seriousness of the problem.
9. Change the subject (e.g., ask for advice to help you solve one of your problems).
10. Express displeasure that the two parties are experiencing conflict (e.g., imply that it might undermine the solidarity of the work group).

Source: adapted from William Morris and Marshall Sashkin, 1976.

Acknowledge that a conflict exists and propose a problem-solving approach for resolving it

It is vital that the mediator takes the problems between conflicting parties seriously. If they feel they have a serious problem, the mediator should not belittle its significance. Remarks like: 'I'm surprised that two intelligent people like you have not been able to work out your disagreement. We have more important things to do here than get all worked up over such petty issues' will make both parties defensive and interfere with any serious problem-solving efforts. While you might wish that your subordinates could have worked out their disagreement without bothering you, this is not the time to lecture them on self-reliance. Inducing guilt feelings by implying personal failure during an already emotional experience tends to distract the participants from the substantive issues at hand.

One early decision a mediator has to make is whether to

convene a joint problem-solving session or to first meet with the parties separately. The diagnostic questions shown in Table 6 should help you weigh up the advantages and disadvantages of each approach.

Table 6 Choosing a format for mediating conflicts

Factors	Hold joint meeting	Hold separate meetings
Awareness and motivation		
■ Both parties are aware of the problem.	Yes	No
■ They are equally motivated to resolve the problem.	Yes	No
■ They accept your legitimacy as a mediator.	Yes	No
Nature of the relationship		
■ The parties hold equal status.	Yes	No
■ They work together regularly.	Yes	No
■ They have a good overall relationship.	Yes	No
Nature of the problem		
■ This is an isolated (not a recurring) problem.	Yes	No
■ The complaint is substantive in nature and easily verified.	Yes	No
■ The parties agree on the root causes of the problem.	Yes	No
■ The parties share common values and work priorities.	Yes	No

The overall methodology for the mediator

1. **What is the current position of the disputants?**
   - Are they both aware a problem exists?
   - Do they agree on the definition of the problem?
   - Are they equally motivated to work on solving the problem?

   The nearer the answer YES is to all three of the questions, the more likely are things to be resolved. If the answer to any of the three questions is NO, then the mediator should work towards some agreement through one-on-one meetings before bringing the disputants together.

2. **What is the current relationship between the disputants?**
   Does their work require them to interact frequently? Is a good
   working relationship critical for their individual job performance? What has their relationship been like in the past? What
   is the difference in their formal status in the organisation? As
   we discussed earlier, joint problem-solving sessions are most
   productive between individuals of equal status who are required
   to work together regularly. This does not mean that joint meetings should not be held between a supervisor and a subordinate,
   only that greater care needs to be taken in preparing for such a
   meeting. Specifically, if a department head becomes involved in
   a dispute between a worker and a supervisor, the department
   head should make sure that the worker does not feel this meeting will serve as an excuse for two managers to gang up on a
   subordinate.

   Separate fact-finding meetings with the disputants before a
   joint meeting are particularly useful when the parties have a
   history of recurring disputes, especially if these disputes should
   have been resolved without a mediator. Such a history often
   suggests a lack of conflict management or problem-solving
   skills on the part of the disputants, or it might stem from a
   broader set of issues that are beyond their control. In these situations, individual coaching sessions before a joint meeting will
   increase your understanding of the root causes and improve the
   individuals' abilities to resolve their differences.

   Following up these private meetings with a joint problem-
   solving session, in which the mediator coaches the disputants
   through the process for resolving their conflicts, can be a positive learning experience.

3. **What is the nature of the problem?** Is the complaint substantive in nature and easily verifiable? If the problem stems
   from conflicting role responsibilities and the actions of both
   parties in question are common knowledge, then a joint problem-solving session can begin on a common information and
   experimental base. In contrast, if the complaint stems from differences in managerial style, values, personality characteristics
   etc., bringing the parties together immediately following a

complaint may seriously undermine the problem-solving process. Complaints that are likely to be interpreted as threats to the self-image of one or both parties (Who am I?, What do I stand for?) warrant considerable individual discussion before a joint meeting is called. To avoid individuals feeling as though they are being ambushed in a meeting, you should discuss serious personal complaints with them ahead of time, in private.

In seeking out the perspective of both parties, maintain a neutral posture regarding the disputants, if not the issues. Effective mediation requires impartiality. If a mediator shows strong personal bias in favour of one party in a joint problem-solving session, the other party may simply get up and walk out. However, this type of personal bias is more likely to creep out in private conversations with the disputants. Statements like, 'I can't believe he really did that!' and 'Everyone seems to be having trouble working with Andrew these days', imply that the mediator is taking sides, and any attempt to appear impartial in a joint meeting will seem like mere window-dressing to appease the other party. No matter how well-intentioned or justified these comments might be, they destroy the credibility of the mediator in the long run. In contrast, the effective mediator respects both parties' points of view and makes sure that both perspectives are expressed adequately.

Occasionally, it is not possible to be impartial on the issues. One person may have violated company policy, engaged in unethical competition with a colleague or broken a personal agreement. In these cases the challenge of the mediator is to separate the offence from the offender. If a person is clearly in the wrong, the inappropriate behaviour needs to be corrected, but in such a way that the individual doesn't feel his or her image and working relationships have been permanently marred. This can be done most effectively when correction occurs in private.

4. **Manage the discussion to insure fairness.** Keep the discussion confined to the issues in hand and do not allow them to stray on to criticism of personalities. The mediator must maintain the role of the problem-solver and not the referee. This is

not to say that strong emotional statements don't have their place. People often associate effective problem-solving with a calm, highly rational discussion of the issues and associate a personality attack with a highly emotional outburst. However, it is important not to confuse affect and effect. Placid, cerebral discussions often don't solve problems, and impassioned statements don't have to be insulting. The critical point about conflict management is that it should be centred on the issues and the consequences of continued conflict on performance. Even when behaviour offensive to one of the parties obviously stems from a personality quirk, the discussion of the problem should be limited to the behaviour. As we stated earlier, attributions about motives or generalisations about specific events or personal proclivities distract participants from the problem-solving process. It is important that the mediator establishes and maintains these ground rules.

It is also important for a mediator to ensure that neither party dominates the discussion. A relatively even balance in the level of inputs improves the quality of the final outcome. It also increases the likelihood that both parties will accept the final decision, because there is a high correlation between feelings about the problem-solving process and attitudes about the final solution. If one party tends to dominate a discussion, the mediator can help balance the exchange by asking the less talkative individual direct questions: 'Now that we have heard Bill's view of that incident, how do you see it?', 'That's an important point, Malcolm, so let's make sure Brian agrees. How do you feel, Brian?'

5. **Facilitate exploration of solutions rather than judge responsibility for the problem.** When the parties must work closely and have a history of chronic interpersonal problems, it is often more important to teach problem-solving skills than to resolve a specific dispute. This is done best when the mediator adopts the posture of facilitator. The role of judge is to render a verdict regarding a problem in the past, not to teach people how to solve their problems in the future. While some disputes obviously involve right and wrong actions, most interpersonal

problems stem from differences in perspective. In these situations it is important that the mediator avoids being seduced into delivering a verdict by comments like, 'Well, you're the boss, tell us which one of us is right', or more subtly, 'I wonder if I did what was right?' The problem with a mediator assuming the role of judge is that it sets in motion processes that are antithetical to effective interpersonal problem-solving. The parties focus on persuading the mediator of their innocence and the other party's guilt rather than striving to improve their working relationship with the assistance of the mediator. The disputants work to establish facts about what happened in the past rather than to reach an agreement about what ought to happen in the future. Consequently, a key aspect of effective mediation is helping the disputants explore multiple alternatives in a non-judgmental manner.

6. **Explore options by focusing on interests, not positions.** Conflict-resolution is often hampered by the perception that where there are incompatible positions there are irreconcilable differences. As noted in the negotiation section, mediation of such conflicts can best be accomplished by examining the interests (goals and concerns) behind the positions. It is these interests that are the driving force behind the positions, and it is these interests that are ultimately what people want satisfied.

It is the job of the mediator to discover where interests meet and where they conflict. Interests tend not to be stated, often because they are unclear to the participants. In order to flesh out each party's interests, ask 'Why' questions: 'Why have they taken this position?', 'Why does this matter to them?' Understand that there is probably no single or simple answer to these questions. For example, each side may represent a number of constituents, each with a special interest.

After each side has articulated its underlying interests, help the parties identify areas of agreement and reconcilability. It is common for participants in an intense conflict to feel that they are on opposite sides of all issues – that they have little in common. Helping them recognise that there are areas of agreement and reconcilability often represents a major turning-point in resolving long-standing feuds.

7. **Make sure that all parties fully understand and support the agreed solution and that follow-up procedures have been established.** Before concluding this discussion of conflict management principles, it is important to briefly mention the last two phases of the problem-solving process: agreement on an action plan and follow-up. These will be discussed within the context of the mediator's role, but they are equally applicable to the other roles.

A common mistake of ineffective mediators is terminating the discussion prematurely. They feel that once the problem has been solved in principle, the disputants can be left to work out the details on their own. Or, they assume that because one of the parties has recommended a solution that appears very reasonable and workable, the second disputant will be willing to implement it. It is very important that when serving as a mediator you insist on a specific plan of action both parties are willing to implement. If you suspect any hesitancy on the part of either disputant, this needs to be explored explicitly (e.g., 'Susan, I sense that you are somewhat less enthusiastic than Jane about this plan. Is there something that bothers you?'). When you are confident that both parties support the plan, you should check to make sure that they are aware of their respective responsibilities and then propose a mechanism for monitoring progress. You might schedule another formal meeting, or you might pop in to both individuals' offices to get a progress report.

Summary

Conflict is a difficult and controversial topic. In Western culture it has negative connotations and we place a high value on getting along with people by being kind and friendly. Although many people understand the value of conflict intellectually, they feel uncomfortable when confronted by it. This discomfort may result from a lack of understanding of the conflict process as well as from a lack of training in ways of handling interpersonal confrontations effectively. This book has addressed these issues by introducing both analytical and behavioural skills. A summary model of conflict management is shown in Figure 3.

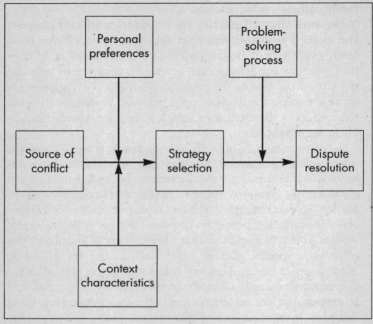

FIGURE 3 Summary model of conflict management

There are basically five approaches to handling conflict:

- Avoiding
- Compromising
- Collaborating
- Forcing
- Accommodating

The model contains three phases: diagnosing the sources of conflict, selecting the appropriate conflict management strategy and using specific problem-solving techniques to effectively resolve interpersonal disputes. The first two phases comprise the diagnostic and analytical aspects of conflict management. Understanding the 'whys' behind confrontations is a key to deciding 'how' to appropriately respond. And skilful implementation is of little value if the wrong approach has been selected. The third phase focuses on the behavioural component of conflict management. The overall philosophy guiding our discussion of conflict is reflected in the implementation segment of the model. We have argued that conflict plays an important role in effective organisations. The operational component of this model focuses on successful resolution of specific disputes and not on eliminating, or preventing, all conflict.

Conflict can be produced by a variety of circumstances: irreconcilable personal differences, discrepancies in information, role incompatibilities and environmentally-induced stress. These causes, and the resulting conflicts, differ in both frequency and intensity. For example, information-based conflicts occur frequently but are easily resolved because the disputants have low personal stakes in the outcome. In contrast, conflicts grounded in differences of perceptions and expectations are generally very intense and difficult to diffuse.

These five approaches to handling conflict reflect different degrees of assertiveness and co-operativeness. There is no best way to handle all conflicts. Instead, in choosing a response mode, managers should consider the quality and duration of the ongoing relationship between the actors, the nature and seriousness of their problem, as well as their personal preferences. Successful strategies need to be set into the context of the overall situation and the overall attitudes, philosophy and personality of the implementor.

The collaborative approach, like the integrative negotiation strategy, generally produces the highest-quality solutions and has the least detrimental effect on relationships. When it is used effectively, all parties tend to be satisfied with the outcome. It takes little skill to impose your authority on another person, to withdraw from a confrontation, to split the difference between opponents or to abandon your position at the slightest sign of opposition, but unfortunately, the collaborative approach can be difficult to implement successfully, particularly in a highly emotional one-to-one situation. Therefore, the behavioural guidelines for resolving an interpersonal confrontation involving complaints and criticisms by using a problem-solving approach has been described in detail. These guidelines include what we have termed 'integrative negotiation tactics' for managing conflict.

Behavioural Guidelines

Effective conflict-management involves both analytical and behavioural elements. First, it is important to understand the true causes of a conflict and to select the appropriate conflict management, or negotiation, approach. Second, it is necessary to effectively implement the approach. The behavioural guidelines for the diagnostic aspects of conflict management include the following:

1. Collect information on the sources of conflict. Identify the source by examining the focus of the dispute. The four sources (and their respective focus) are: personal differences (perception and expectations); information deficiency (misinformation and misinterpretation); role incompatibility (goals and responsibilities); environmental stress (resource scarcity and uncertainty).

2. Utilise the collaborative approach for managing conflict, including integrative negotiation tactics, unless specific conditions dictate the use of an alternative approach.

3. Use the forcing approach only when: the issue is extremely important to you; a close, ongoing relationship is not necessary; you have much more power than the other person; there is a high sense of urgency.

4. Use the accommodating approach only when: the issue is not important to you; a close, ongoing relationship is critical; you have no other option (low power); time is not a factor.

5. Use the compromising approach only when: the issue is very complex and of moderate importance to both parties (and the parties feel strongly about different aspects of the issues); the relationship is of moderate importance; the parties have relatively equal power; time constraints are low.

6. Use the avoiding approach only when: the issue is not important to you; the relationship is not critical; your relative power is equal to high; time is not a factor.

The behavioural guidelines for effectively implementing the collaborative (problem-solving) approach to conflict management are summarised below. These are organised according to three roles. Guidelines for the problem-identification and solution-generation phases of the problem-solving process are specified for each role. Guidelines for the action plan and follow-up phases are the same for all three roles.

The First Party – The Initiator

Problem Identification
1. Describe your problem briefly and clearly in terms of behaviours, consequences and feelings.

('When you do X, Y happens and I feel Z.')
- Maintain personal ownership of the problem
- Use a specific incident to illustrate the expectations or standards violated
- Stick to the facts, avoid drawing evaluative conclusions and attributing motives to the respondent

2. Persist until understood and encourage two-way discussion.
   - Restate your concerns or give additional examples
   - Avoid introducing additional issues or letting your frustration sour your emotional tone
   - Invite the respondent to ask questions and express another perspective

3. Manage the agenda carefully.
   - Approach multiple problems incrementally – proceeding from simple to complex, easy to hard, concrete to abstract
   - Conversely, don't become fixated on one issue. If you reach an impasse, expand the discussion to increase the likelihood of an integrative outcome

Solution Generation
4. Make a request.
   - Focus on those things you have in common (principles, goals, constraints) as the basis for recommending preferred alternatives

The Second Party – The 'Accused'

Problem Identification
1. Establish a climate for joint problem-solving.
   - Show genuine concern and interest; respond empathetically, even if you disagree with the complaint
   - Respond appropriately to the initiator's emotions; if necessary, allow the person to 'let off steam' before addressing the complaint

2. Seek additional information about the problem.
   - Ask questions that channel the initiator's statements from general to specific and from evaluative to descriptive

3. Agree with some aspect of the complaint.
   - Signal your willingness to consider making changes by agreeing with facts, perceptions, feelings or principles

Solution Generation

4. Ask for recommendations.
   - To avoid debating the merits of a single suggestion, brainstorm multiple alternatives

The Mediator

Problem Identification

1. Acknowledge that a conflict exists.
   - Select the most appropriate setting (one-to-one conference vs. group meeting) for coaching and fact-finding
   - Propose a problem-solving approach for resolving the dispute

2. Maintain a neutral posture.
   - Assume the role of facilitator, not judge. Do not belittle the problem or berate the disputants for their inability to resolve their differences
   - Be impartial towards the disputants and the issues (as long as policy has not been violated)
   - If correction is necessary, do it in private

3. Manage the discussion to ensure fairness.
   - Focus discussion on the conflict's impact on performance and the detrimental effect of a continued conflict
   - Keep the discussion issue-oriented, not personality-oriented
   - Do not allow one party to dominate the discussion; ask directed questions to maintain balance

Solution Generation

4. Explore options by focusing on the interests behind stated positions.
   - Explore the 'whys' behind disputants' arguments/claims
   - Help disputants see commonalities among their goals, values and principles
   - Use commonalities to generate multiple alternatives
   - Maintain a non-judgemental manner

All Roles

Action Plan and Follow-Up

1. Ensure that all parties support the agreed plan.
   - Verify understanding of, and commitment to, specific actions

2. Establish a mechanism for follow-up.
   - Create benchmarks for measuring progress and ensuring accountability
   - Encourage flexibility in adjusting the plan to meet emerging circumstances

Skill Analysis

Case Involving Interpersonal Conflict
Health Provisions Limited

Health Provisions Limited (HPL) provided one of the first private health-care schemes to the British market. The founders had all worked in the National Health Service in some capacity and retained a conservative philosophy to the business, putting patient care very high on their list of priorities. Their main business was providing employee cover for blue-chip companies, and they kept out of the more competitive direct-consumer-marketing approach of the growing number of rivals. Until very recently they felt secure and in a good position to handle further changes in the economic and political environment.

Carolyn Richardson was one of the founders of HPL and is highly respected in the profession. The other partners, comfortable with Carolyn's conservative, yet flexible nature, elected her to the position of the first managing director.

After that, Carolyn became known as 'the great equaliser'. She worked hard to make sure that all the partners were included in decisions and that strong relations were maintained. Her management philosophy was built on the concept of trust and loyalty – loyalty to the organisation, loyalty to its members, loyalty to friends and, most of all, loyalty to the clients.

As the total market grew, various overseas-funded health-care groups began to encroach on HPL's client base and its growth increasingly failed to keep pace with those of its rivals. As a result, Carolyn has reluctantly begun to consider the merits of more aggressive promotion and moving into direct selling.

One evening Carolyn talked about her concern with her bridge partner and life-long friend, Susan Ross who owned a private hospital developed in conjunction with HPL. Everyone respected Susan for her knowledge, work rate and uncanny ability to predict trends. Susan knew what to do and when to do it and her present preoccupation was modifying her hospital group for long-term mental-health patients.

When Susan heard Carolyn's concerns and need for an aggressive approach, she suggested to her friend that what HPL needed was some fresh blood, someone who could infuse enthusiasm into the organisation. She suggested a friend who had worked in health-care in Canada and 'was good at sorting things out – if a bit abrasive'. The friend's name was Mark Western.

Carolyn suggested the idea of employing Mark at the next staff meeting, but it was met with caution and scepticism. 'Yes, he's had a brilliant career on paper,' said one senior partner, 'but he's never stayed in one place long enough to really finish what he has started. Look at his CV. During the past seven years, he's been with four different organisations.'

'That's true,' said Carolyn, 'but his references are really good. In fact, he's been described as a rising star, aggressive and productive. He's just what we need to help us explore new opportunities.'

Throughout the discussion, Carolyn defended Mark's record and pointed to his impressive performance. She deflected concerns about his reputation by saying that he had been recommended by a loyal and trusted friend. Eventually, the other partners agreed, albeit reluctantly, to recruit Mark.

When Carolyn offered Mark the job, he was promised the freedom to work out his own ideas.

Mark worked hard, regaining corporate clients and developing telephone-selling techniques for smaller companies and individuals. He set HLP on the road to recovery and was liked by many of the junior staff as a breath of fresh air. He was open to new ideas and was exciting to work with. His abrasive manner confused and annoyed the other partners who thought Mark was attempting to move things too quickly. It was not uncommon for sharp disagreements to erupt in staff meetings, but Carolyn tried to smooth ruffled feathers and maintain a productive atmosphere.

Mark seemed oblivious to all the turmoil he was causing. He was optimistic about potential growth opportunities. His main idea was similar to Susan Ross's – he thought that the group should go into long-term care of the mentally ill using the generous government grants now available – 'If we don't, then the others will steal a march on us and we will be stuck doing what we do now for ever with smaller and smaller margins.'

Months passed and dissension among the managers grew. Mark's frustration over the lack of support among the senior partners began to undermine the day-to-day operations of HPL. He began to criticise his detractors in discussions with younger HPL employees. In addition, he moved staff away from the core business into his own and as yet unproven scheme.

Amid a rapidly spreading undercurrent of tension, one of the founding partners, Neville Watson, approached Carolyn one day.

'Carolyn, I speak for most of the senior staff when I say we are very troubled by Mark's approach. We've expressed ourselves well enough for Mark to understand, but his actions defy everything we've said. He's a catastrophe just waiting to happen.'

'You are right, Neville,' replied Carolyn. 'I'm troubled, too. We have an opportunity to attract new business with some of Mark's new ideas. And the younger staff love working on his projects. But he has stirred up a lot of turmoil.'

Neville agreed. 'The real issue is that HPL is no longer presenting a unified image. Mark is wilfully defying the stated objectives of our organisation. And some of our oldest clients don't like that. There is real concern about the sort of patients Mark's ideas will produce. They just won't mix with our existing people.'

'That's true, Neville. However, some of the clients think he is a breath of fresh air. He does have a reputation for being right.'

'Come on, Carolyn. You and I both know that we must not risk our reputation and our core business in this way. Mark must be made to understand that or go. I'm sorry, I don't like speaking this way but the other partners agree.'

Carolyn realised she faced the most difficult challenge of her career. She felt a strong personal investment in helping Mark succeed, having personally recruited him and been his ally in the early days. Carolyn was also haunted by her promise to Mark that he would have the freedom and flexibility to perform as he pleased. However, this flexibility had clearly caused problems.

Reluctantly, Carolyn called Mark in for a meeting, hoping to find some basis for compromise.

Carolyn: 'I gather you know the kinds of concerns the senior partners have expressed regarding your approach.'

Mark: 'I suppose you've talked with Neville. Well, we did have a small disagreement earlier this week.'

Carolyn: 'The way Neville tells it, you're moving staff about without any form of discussion and the core business is suffering – he has tried to discuss it with you and you simply ignored him and went ahead. He is a senior partner and he calls it dangerous insubordination.'

Mark: 'Well, it's just like Watson to see progressive change as an attempt to take away his power.'

Carolyn: 'It's not quite that simple, Mark. When we founded HPL, we all agreed that a conservative stance was best. And right now, with the economic indicators looking soft, many experts agree that it may still be the best alternative.'

Mark: 'Carolyn, what are you going to rely on – predictions or performance? Old views need to be challenged and ultimately discarded. How else are we going to progress and keep up with our competitors?'

Carolyn: 'I agree we need to change, Mark, but gradually. Your ideas are good, but you have to have patience. You also have to take the people that matter with you. Its the way you try and do things. You make people defensive.'

Mark: 'You're telling me. And at this rate, it doesn't make much difference which direction we're heading.'

Carolyn: 'Come on, Mark, you are making things very difficult for yourself and me. They do have a point in saying that the presence of long-term mental patients will antagonise our existing clients. The sums sound fine, but you have to convince everyone – work with them and not against them – you could be wrong. The way ahead is likely to be a compromise and the way we are going now, compromise seems a million miles off.'

Mark's emotions betray his impatience with the pace of the organisation and he becomes agitated.

Mark: 'I've admired your enthusiasm and I value your advice but I honestly think you're kidding yourself. You seem to think you can get things done without ruffling a few feathers. Are you interested in appearance or substance? If you want appearance, then hire a good PR person. If you want substance, then back me up.'

Carolyn: 'Mark , it simply isn't that easy. I'm not HPL, I'm simply its caretaker. You know we make decisions around here by consensus; that's the backbone of this organisation. To move ahead, the confidence of the others has to be won, especially that of the partners. Frankly your attitude is one of the main problems.'

Mark: 'You promised me flexibility and autonomy. I'm not getting that any more, Carolyn . All I'm getting is grief.'

Carolyn: 'That may be true. But your whole approach . . .'

Mark: 'Oh, yes, I thought you would get onto that. The sports car, the bachelor lifestyle, the messy office. But, again, that's appearance, Carolyn, not substance. Performance is what counts. That's what got me this far. You know I could walk out of here and sell my ideas to any other group – and for more money.'

Carolyn: 'Wow, slow down.'

Mark: 'Do you honestly believe this can be salvaged? I don't think so. Maybe it's time for me to move on. Isn't that why you called me in here anyway?'

Carolyn, feeling uncomfortable, breaks eye contact and shifts her gaze to the London skyline. After a long pause, she continues, still gazing out of the window.

Carolyn: 'I don't know, Mark. I feel I've failed. My grand experiment in change has polarised the office; we've a war out there. On one hand, you really have done a good job here. HPL will no doubt lose a good part of its customer base if you leave. You have created a good atmosphere in your department – customers and staff. If you go we will lose all that, and the chance to change.'

Mark: 'It's just like you Carolyn to take this problem personally. You take everything personally. Even when I beat you at squash. Your heart's in the right place but you just can't ever seem to go for the jugular. You know and I know that HPL needs change. But it doesn't appear to be ready for it yet. And I'm certainly not willing to move slowly.'

Carolyn: 'Yes. Perhaps. It's just hard to give up... [long pause]. OK forget it.'

Mark: 'Fine.'

Discussion Questions

1. What are the sources of conflict in this case?
2. What approaches to conflict-management are used by the people in this situation? How effective was each approach?
3. Based on the behavioural guidelines for the collaborative approach, how could Carolyn have managed this conflict more effectively?

Skill Practice

Exercises in Selecting an Appropriate Conflict-Management Strategy

Background
Not all conflicts are alike, therefore they should not all be managed in exactly the same way. Effective managers are not only able to properly assess the true cause(s) of conflict; in addition, they are able to properly match the type of conflict with the appropriate management strategy.

Assignment
For each of the following brief scenarios, select the most appropriate conflict–management strategy below. Refer to Table 7 for assistance in matching situational factors with strategies.

- Forcing
- Accommodating
- Compromising
- Collaborating
- Avoiding

Table 7 Matching the conflict-management approach with the situation

Situational considerations	Conflict-management approach				
	Forcing	Accommo-dating	Compro-mising	Collabo-rating	Avoiding
Issue importance	High	Low	Med	High	Low
Relationship importance	Low	High	Med	High	Low
Relative power	High	Low	Equal-high	Low-high	Equal-high
Time pressure	Med-high	Med-high	Low	Low	Med-high

Argyll Steakhouse

You have decided to take your family out to the local steak house, Argyll Steakhouse, for dinner to celebrate your son's birthday. You are a single parent, so getting home from work in time to prepare a nice dinner is very difficult. On entering the restaurant, you ask the waiter to seat you in the non-smoking section because your daughter, Sheila, is allergic to tobacco smoke. On your way to your seat, you notice that the restaurant seems crowded for a Monday night.

After you and your children are seated and have placed your orders, your conversation turns to the family plans for the approaching Christmas holidays. Suddenly you notice that your daughter is sneezing and her eyes are beginning to water. You look around and see a lively group of businessmen seated at the table behind you, all of whom are smoking. Your impression is that they are celebrating a special occasion. Looking back at Sheila, you realise that something has got to be done quickly. You ask your son to take Sheila outside while you go and find the waiter.

1. The salient situational factors are _____
2. The most appropriate conflict-management strategy is _____
_____

Please refer to the Scoring Key at the end of the book (page 90) for an example of how this particular scenario could be tabled.

Avocado Computers

Your name is Bran Greenway. When the head of Avocado Computers ran into production problems with its new automated production line, you were lured from Western Computers – a competitor. It meant a significant increase in pay and the opportunity to manage a state-of-the-art production plant. What's more, there were very few other female production managers in the region. You've been in the post for a year, and it's been exciting to see your staff start working together as a team to solve problems, improve quality and finally get the plant up to capacity. In general, Robert, the owner, has also been a plus. He is energetic, fair and a proven industry leader. You feel fortunate to be in a coveted position, in a 'star' firm, in a growth industry.

However, there is one distraction that annoys you. Robert has an obsession with cleanliness, order and appearance. He wants all the robots painted the same colour, the components within the computer laid out perfectly on a grid, the workers wearing clean overalls and the floor 'clean enough to eat off'. You are worried by this compulsion. 'It might impress potential clients when they tour the production facility, but is it all that important? After all, who's ever going to look at the inside of their computer? Why should customers care about the colour of the robot that built their computers? And who, for heaven's sake, would ever want to have a picnic in a factory?'

Today is your first yearly performance appraisal interview with Robert. In preparation for the meeting, he has sent you a memo outlining 'Areas of strength' and 'Areas of concern'. You look with pride at the number of items listed in the first column. It's obvious that Robert likes your work. But you are a bit annoyed at the single item of concern: 'Needs to maintain a cleaner facility, including employee appearance'. You mull this 'demerit' over in your mind, wrestling with how to respond in your interview.

1. The salient situational factors are _____
2. The most appropriate conflict-management strategy is _____

_____

Phelan Ltd

You are Philip Jameson, the head of sales for an office products firm, Phelan Ltd. Your sales personnel sell primarily to small businesses in Scotland. Phelan's performance is about average for this rapidly-growing market. The firm's new president, James Owen, is putting a lot of pressure on you to increase sales. You feel that a major obstacle is the firm's policy on extending credit. Celia, the head of the credit office, insists that all new customers fill out an extensive credit application. Credit risks must be low; credit terms and collection procedures are tough. You can appreciate her point of view, but you feel it is unrealistic. Your competitors already are much more lenient in their credit examinations, they extend credit to higher risks, their credit terms are more favourable, and they are less aggressive in collecting overdue payments. Your sales personnel frequently complain that they aren't playing on a 'level playing field' with their competitors. When you brought this concern to James, he said he wanted you and Celia to work things out. His instructions didn't give many clues to his priorities on this matter. You realise the need to increase sales, but the small business failure is alarming, so you want to be careful that you don't make bad credit decisions.

You decide it's time to have a serious discussion with Celia. A lot is at stake.

1. The salient situational factors are _____

2. The most appropriate conflict-management strategy is _____ _____

Exercises in Resolving Interpersonal Disputes

Background
The heart of conflict-management is resolving intense, emotionally-charged confrontations. We have extensively discussed guidelines for utilising the collaborative (problem-solving) approach to conflict-management in these situations. Assuming that the collaborative approach is appropriate for a particular situation, the general guidelines can be used by an initiator, a responder or a mediator.

Assignment
The following are three situations involving interpersonal conflict and disagreement. The instructions at the beginning of each situation will explain the assignment. The wording of the assignment refers to work in large or medium sized groups.

Where's My Speech?

Instructions
- Divide the main group into sub-groups of three.
- Choose two members who will take the roles of Janet as the initiator and Sarah as the respondent – making sure that each

does not read the other's brief. The third member of the group acts initially as an observer working with the Observer's Feedback form to be found at the end of the book (page 91).

■ Run the role play for not more than 15 minutes and at the end allow the observer to give feedback for a similar time.

If the role play has not reached a satisfactory resolution

■ Continue the role play from the point previously reached, using the observer as a mediator.

■ Discuss what has happened using the Observer's Feedback form

■ Discuss where in Beacon Lights organisation a mediator might be found, and the consequences of failing to find one in time.

■ Present to the whole group: (1) What went well in your role plays. (2) What went badly. (3) The key learning points for you.

Brief for Janet, Director of Personnel, Beacon Lights

You have been director of personnel for Beacon Lights for ten years. Just when you thought you had everything under control, disaster struck. You have just heard that a former employee is suing the company for unfair dismissal, the sales director was forced to resign last month because of the company's poor performance, and your secretary just died of a heart attack.

You have been asked to give a speech at a seminar on a new productivity programme your company has pioneered, and you are looking forward to getting away from the office for a few days to catch your breath. You dictated your speech to your new secretary, Sarah, a couple of days ago so that she would have plenty of time to get it typed and reproduced.

This morning you have come into the office to proof-read and rehearse your speech before catching the midday train, and you are shocked to find a sick note from your secretary. You rush over to her desk and frantically begin searching for your speech notes. You find them mixed up with some material for the quarterly report that should have been completed two weeks ago, a stack of overdue correspondence and two days' unopened post.

As you dial your secretary's home phone number, you realise

that you are perspiring heavily and your face is flushed. This is the biggest disaster you can remember happening in years.

Brief for Sarah, Secretary

You hear the phone ring, and it is all you can do to get out of bed and limp into the kitchen to answer it. You feel dreadful. Last night, you slipped on your son's skateboard in the drive and sprained your knee. You can hardly move today and the pain is excruciating. You are also reluctant to answer the phone because you know it is probably your boss, Janet, who will be moaning about your work rate. You realise you deserve some of the blame, but it isn't all your fault. Since you began working for Janet a month ago, you have asked several times for a thorough job description. You find you don't really understand either Janet's priorities or your specific responsibilities. You are replacing a woman who died suddenly after working for Janet for ten years. You have found working with Janet extremely frustrating. She has been too busy to train you properly and she assumes you know as much about the job as your predecessor. This is particularly a problem since you haven't worked as a secretary for three years and you feel your skills are a bit rusty.

Janet's speech is a good example of the difficulties you have experienced. She gave you the notes a couple of days ago and said it was urgent, but that was on top of a quarterly report that was already overdue, a backlog of correspondence, filing and more. You have never compiled a report like this before, and every time you asked Janet a question she said she'd discuss it with you later and promptly ran off to another meeting. When you asked for some additional help to catch up on the overdue work, Janet said the company couldn't afford it because of poor sales. This annoyed you because you know you are being paid far less than your predecessor. You knew Janet faced some urgent deadlines, so you had planned to return to the office last night to type her speech and try to complete the report, but two hours in the waiting room at the hospital put an end to that plan. You tried calling Janet to explain the problem only to find out that her home number is ex-directory.

You sit down, prop up your leg and wince with pain as you pick up the phone.

Can Harry Fit In?

Instructions
■ Divide the main group into sub-groups of three.
■ Choose two members who will take the roles of Harry as the initiator and Margaret as the respondent – making sure that each does not read the other's brief. The third member of the group acts initially as an observer working the Observer's Feedback form to be found at the end of the book (page 91).
■ Run the role play for not more than 15 minutes and then allow the observer to give feedback for a similar time.

If the role play has not reached a satisfactory resolution
■ Continue the role play from the point previously reached, using the observer as a mediator.
■ Discuss what has happened using the Observer's Feedback form
■ Discuss where in the auditing team a mediator could be found, and the consequences of not finding such a person.
■ Present to the whole group: (1) What went well in your role plays. (2) What went badly. (3) The key learning points.

Brief for Margaret, Office Manager
You are the manager of an auditing team sent to Bangkok, Thailand, to represent a major international accounting firm with headquarters in Zurich, Switzerland. You and Harry, one of your auditors, were sent to Bangkok to set up an auditing operation. Harry is seven years older than you and has been with the firm five years longer. Your relationship has become strained since you were recently appointed office manager. You feel you were given the post because you have established an excellent working relationship with the Thai staff as well as a broad range of international clients. But Harry has told other members of the staff that your promotion simply reflects the firm's heavy emphasis on 'Yes' people. He has tried to isolate you from the all-male accounting staff by focusing discussions on sports, local night-spots, etc.

You are sitting in your office reading some complicated new reporting procedures which have just arrived from head office. Your concentration is suddenly interrupted by a loud knock on your door. Without waiting for an invitation to enter, Harry bursts into your office. He is obviously very upset, and you already know why he is in such a nasty mood. You recently posted the audit assignments for next month, and you scheduled Harry for a job you knew he wouldn't like. Harry is one of your senior auditors and the company norm is that choice assignments go with seniority. This particular job will require him to spend two weeks away from Bangkok in a remote town, working with a company with notoriously messy records.

Unfortunately, you have had to assign several of these less desirable audits to Harry recently because you are short of personnel. But that's not the only reason. You have received a number of complaints from the junior staff (all Thais) that Harry treats them in a condescending manner. They feel he is always looking for an opportunity to boss them around, as if he were their supervisor instead of an experienced, supportive mentor. As a result, your whole operation works more smoothly when you can send Harry out of town on a solo project for several days. It keeps him from coming into your office and telling you how to do your job, and the morale of the rest of the auditing staff is significantly higher.

Harry slams the door and proceeds to express his anger over this assignment.

Brief for Harry, Senior Auditor

You are really fed up! Margaret is deliberately trying to undermine your status in the office. She knows that the company tradition is that senior auditors get the better jobs. And this isn't the first time this has happened. Since her promotion she has tried to keep you out of the office as much as possible. It's as if she doesn't want her rival for leadership of the office around. When you were asked to go to Bangkok, you assumed that you would be made the office manager because of your seniority in the firm. You are certain that the decision to pick Margaret is yet another indication of positive discrimination against white males.

In staff meetings, Margaret has talked about the need to be

sensitive to the feelings of the office staff as well as the clients in this multi-cultural setting. She's got a nerve to be preaching about sensitivity! 'What about my feelings, for heaven's sake?' you wonder. This is nothing more than a straightforward power play. She is probably feeling insecure about being the only female accountant in the office and being promoted over someone with more experience. 'Sending me out of town,' you decide, 'is a clear case of out of sight, out of mind.'

Well, it's not going to happen that easily. You are not going to roll over and let her treat you unfairly. It's time for a showdown. If she doesn't agree to change this assignment and apologise for the way she's been treating you, you're going to register a formal complaint with her boss in Zurich. You are prepared to submit your resignation if the situation doesn't improve.

Meeting at Hartford Manufacturing Company

Instructions
- Divide into sub-groups of five.
- Choose one observer and four people to play the main characters – Peter Smith, Richard Hootten, Barbara Price and Chris Jones. The person playing the role of Peter Smith, and nobody else, should read the letters shown as exhibits 1, 2 and 3 (pages 76–78) – although he may chose to share them during the meeting. No characters should read other people's roles.
- The obsever should watch the meeting using the Observer's Feedback form found in the back of the book (page 91).
- Run the role play for not more than 30 minutes and allow the observer to give feedback using the Observer's form for a similar time.

If the role play has not reached a satisfactory resolution
- Continue the role play from the point previously reached, using the observer as mediator.
- Discuss what has happened and present to the whole group: (1) What went well. (2) What went badly. (3) Key learning points.

Background

Hartford Manufacturing Company is the largest subsidiary of Riding Industries. Since its formation in 1918, Hartford Manufacturing has become an industrial leader in the UK. Its sales currently average approximately £25 million a year, with an annual growth of approximately six per cent. There are over 850 employees in production, sales and marketing, accounting, engineering and management.

Peter Smith has been managing director for two years and is well-respected by his subordinates. He has the reputation of being firm but fair. Peter's training in college was in engineering, so he is technically-minded, and he frequently likes to walk around the production area to see for himself how things are going. He has also been known to roll up his sleeves and help work on a problem on the shop floor. He is not opposed to rubbing shoulders with even the lowest-level employees. On the other hand, he tries to run a tight company. He holds high expectations for performance, especially from those in managerial positions.

Richard Hooton is the director of production at Hartford Manufacturing. He has been with the company since he was 19. He has worked himself up through the ranks and now at the age of 54 he is the oldest manager. Hooton has his own ideas of how things should be run in production and he is reluctant to tolerate any intervention from anyone, even Peter Smith. Because he has been with the company so long, he feels he knows it better than anyone else, and he believes he has had a hand in making it the success that it is. His main goal is to keep production running smoothly and efficiently.

Barbara Price is the director of sales and marketing. She joined the company about 18 months ago after completing her MBA at Keele. She previously held the position of assistant manager of marketing at Riding Industries. Price is a very conscientious employee and is anxious to make a name for herself. Her major objective, which she has never hesitated to make public, is to be a general manager one day. Sales at Hartford Manufacturing have increased in the past year to near-record levels under her guidance.

Christopher Jones is the regional sales manager for the

Yorkshire region. He reports directly to Barbara Price. The Yorkshire region represents the largest market for Hartford Manufacturing, and Jones is considered the most competent salesperson in the company. He has built personal relationships with several major clients in his region, and it appears that some sales occur as much because of Christopher Jones as because of the products of Hartford Manufacturing. Jones has been with the company 12 years, all of them in sales.

This is Friday afternoon and tomorrow Peter Smith leaves for Copenhagen to attend an important meeting with potential overseas investors. He will be gone for two weeks. Before he leaves, there are several items in his in-tray that must receive attention. He calls a meeting with Richard Hooton and Barbara Price in his office. Just before the meeting begins, Christopher Jones calls and asks if he may join the meeting for a few minutes since he is at head office and has something important to discuss. It involves both Peter Smith and Richard Hooton. Smith gives permission for him to join the meeting as there may not be another chance to meet Jones before the trip. The meeting convenes with Smith, Hooton, Price and Jones all in the room.

Brief for Peter Smith, Managing Director

Three letters arrived today and you judge them to be sufficiently important to require your attention before you leave on your trip (see exhibits 1, 2, and 3). Each letter represents a problem that requires immediate action, and you need commitments from key staff members to resolve these problems. You are concerned about this meeting, because these individuals don't work as well together as you'd like.

For example, Richard Hooton tends to be very difficult to pin down. He always seems suspicious of the motives of others and has a reputation for not making tough decisions. You sometimes wonder how a person could become the head of production in a major manufacturing firm by avoiding controversial issues and blaming others for the results.

In contrast, Barbara Price is very straightforward. You always know exactly where she stands. The problem is that sometimes she doesn't take enough time to study a problem before making a

Exhibit 1

T.J. WRIGHT
Chartered Accountants
Chorley Road
Birmingham

10 February 1994
Mr Peter Smith
Managing Director
Hartford Manufacturing Company
Chorley Industrial Estate
Birmingham

Dear Mr Smith

As you requested last month, we have now completed our
audit of Hartford Manufacturing Company. We find
accounting procedures and fiscal control to be very
satisfactory. A more detailed report of these matters is
attached. However, we did discover during our perusal of
company records that the production department has
consistently incurred cost overruns during the past two
quarters. Cost per unit of production is approximately
5 per cent over budget. While this is not a serious
problem given the financial solvency of your company,
we thought it wise to bring it your attention.

Yours sincerely

Trevor J Wright

Exhibit 2

BAILDON INDUSTRIES
New Hall Way
Bradford
West Yorkshire

Mr Peter Smith   8 February 1994
Managing Director
Hartford Manufacturing Company
Chorley Industrial Estate
Birmingham

Dear Mr Smith

We have been purchasing your products since 1975 and we have been very satisfied with our relations with your sales personnel.

Unfortunately this is no longer the case. Your sales representative for the Bradford area, Sam Sneddon, has looked like and smelled like he was under the influence of alcohol on the last three occasions he has appeared on our premises. Not only that, but our last order was mistakenly recorded, so we received the wrong quantity of products.

I'm sure you don't make it a practice to put your company's reputation in the hands of someone like Sam Sneddon, so I suggest you get someone else to cover this area. We cannot tolerate, and I am sure that other companies in the Bradford area cannot tolerate, this kind of relationship to continue. While we judge your products to be excellent, we will be forced to find other sources if some action is not taken.

Yours sincerely

David Stokoe
Purchasing Manager

Exhibit 3

HARTFORD MANUFACTURING COMPANY
CHORLEY INDUSTRIAL ESTATE
BIRMINGHAM
A subsidiary of Riding Industries

Memorandum
TO: Peter Smith, Managing Director
FROM: Barbara Price, Sales and Marketing Director
DATE: 11 February 1994

Mr Smith:
        In response to your concerns, we have instituted several incentive programmes among our sales force to increase sales during these traditionally slow months. We have set up competition among regions with the sales people in the top region being recognised in the company newsletter and presented with engraved plaques. We have introduced a 'holiday in America' award for the top salesperson in the company and we have instituted cash bonuses for any salesperson who gets a new customer order. However, these incentives have now been operating for a month and sales haven't increased at all. In fact, in two regions they have decreased by an average of 5 per cent.
        What do you suggest now? We have promised that these incentives will continue to run for the rest of this quarter, but they seem to be doing no good. Not only that, but we cannot afford to provide the incentives within our current budget, and unless sales increase, we will be in the red. **Regretfully, I recommend dropping the programme.**

decision. She tends to be impulsive and anxious to make a decision, whether it's the right one or not. Her general approach to resolving disagreements between departments is to seek expedient compromises. You are particularly disturbed by her approach to the sales-incentive problem. You felt strongly that something needed to be done to increase sales during the winter months. You reluctantly agreed to the incentive programme because you didn't want to dampen her initiative. But you aren't convinced this is the right answer, because frankly, you're not sure what the real problem is, yet!

Christopher Jones is an aggressive sales manager. He is hard-driving and sometimes ruffles the feathers of other members of staff with his uncompromising, 'black-and-white' style. He is also fiercely loyal to his sales staff, so you're certain he'll take the complaint about Sam Sneddon personally.

In contrast to the styles of your colleagues, you have tried to utilise an integrative approach to problem-solving, focusing on the facts, treating everyone's inputs equally, and keeping conversations about controversial topics problem-focused. One of your goals since taking over this position two years ago is to foster a team approach within your staff.

(Note: For more information about how you might approach the issues raised by these letters in your staff meeting, review the collaborating approach in Table 2 (page 19) as well as the mediator's behavioural guidelines at the end of the Skill Learning section (page 53).)

Brief to Richard Hooton, Director of Production

The backbone of Hartford Manufacturing is production. You have watched the company grow from a small, struggling factory to a thriving business, built on outstanding production processes. Your own reputation among those who know manufacturing is a good one, and you are confident that you have been a major factor in the success of Hartford Manufacturing. You have turned down several job offers over the years because you feel loyal to the company, but sometimes the younger employees don't seem to afford you the respect that you think you deserve.

The only time you have major problems in production is when

the young know-it-alls fresh from college have come in and tried to change things. With their scientific management concepts and fuzzy-headed human relations training, they have more often made a mess of things. The best production methods have been practised for years in the company, and you have yet to see anyone who could improve on your system.

On the other hand, you have respect for Peter Smith as the managing director. He has lots of experience and the right kind of training, and he is also involved in the production side of the organisation. He has often given you good advice but he usually lets you do what you feel is best and he rarely dictates specific methods for doing things.

Your general approach to problems is to avoid controversy. You feel uncomfortable when production is made the scapegoat for problems in the company. Just because this is a manufacturing business, it seems as if everyone tries to pin the blame for problems on the production department. You've felt for years that the firm was getting away from what it does best – mass-producing a few standard products. Instead, the trend has been for marketing and sales to push for more and more products, shorter lead times, and greater customisation capability. These actions have increased costs and caused incredible production delays as well as higher reject rates.

(Note: During the impending meeting, you should adopt the avoidance approach shown in Table 2, page 19. Defend your territory, place blame on others, defer taking a stand and avoid taking responsibility for making a controversial decision.)

Brief for Barbara Price, Director of Sales and Marketing

You are anxious to impress Peter Smith because you have your eye on a position in the parent company, Riding Industries, that is opening up at the end of the year. It would mean a promotion for you. A positive recommendation from Peter Smith would carry a lot of weight in the selection process. Given that both Hartford Manufacturing and Riding Industries are largely male dominated, you are pleased with your career progress so far, and you are hoping to keep it up.

One current concern is the suggestion of Peter Smith some

time ago that you look into the problem of slow sales during the winter months. You implemented an incentive plan that was highly recommended by an industry analyst at a recent trade conference. It consists of three separate incentive programmes: (1) competition among regions in which the salesperson in the top region would have their picture in the company newsletter and receive engraved plaques, (2) a holiday in America for the top salesperson in the company, and (3) cash bonuses for salespeople who obtained new customer orders. The trouble is, these incentives haven't worked. Not only have sales not increased for the company as a whole, but two of the regions are down by an average of five per cent. You have told the sales force that the incentives will continue in this quarter, but if sales don't improve, your budget will be in the red. You haven't budgeted for the prizes, since you expected the increased sales to more than offset the cost of the incentives.

Obviously this was a bad idea and it isn't working, therefore it should be dropped immediately. You are a bit embarrassed about this aborted project. But it is better to cut your losses and try something else rather than supporting an obvious loser.

In general, you are very confident and self-assured. You feel that the best way to get work done is through negotiation and compromise. What's important is making a decision quickly and efficiently. Maybe everyone doesn't get exactly what they want, but at least they can get on with their work. There are no absolutes in this business, only 'greys' that can be traded off to keep the management process from being bogged down with 'paralysis by analysis'. You are impatient over delays caused by intensive studies and investigations of detail. You agree with Tom Peters: action is the hallmark of successful managers.

(Note: During this meeting, use the compromise approach shown in Table 2, page 19. Do whatever is necessary to help the group make a quick decision so you can get on with the pressing demands of your work.)

Brief for Christopher Jones, Regional Sales Manager
You don't go to company headquarters very often because your customer contacts take up most of your time. You regularly work

50 to 60 hours a week and you are proud of the job you do. You also feel a special obligation to your customers to provide them with the best product available in the most timely fashion. This sense of obligation comes not only from your commitment to the company but also from your personal relationships with many of the customers.

Recently, you have been receiving more and more complaints about late deliveries. The time lag between ordering and delivery is increasing, and some customers have been greatly inconvenienced by the delays. You have sent a formal inquiry to production to find out what the problem is. They replied that they are producing as efficiently as possible and they see nothing wrong with past practices. The assistant to Richard Hooton even suggested that this was just another example of the sales force's unrealistic expectations.

Not only will sales be negatively affected if these delays continue, but your reputation with your customers will be damaged. You have promised them that the problem will be quickly solved and that products will begin arriving on time. Since Richard Hooton is such a rigid person, however, you are almost certain that it will do no good to talk to him. His subordinate probably got his negative attitude from Hooton.

In general, Hooton is a 1960s production worker who is being pulled by the rest of the firm into the new age of the 1990s. Competition is different, technology is different and management is different. You need shorter lead times, a wider range of products and the capacity to do some customised work. Admittedly, this makes production's work harder, but other firms are providing these services with the use of just-in-time management processes, robots etc. But Hooton is reluctant to change.

Instead of getting down to the real problems, head office, in their typical high-handed fashion, announced an incentives plan. This implies that the problem is in the field, not the factory. It made some of your people angry to think they were being pressed to increase their efforts when they weren't receiving the back-up support they required. They liked the prizes, but the way the plan was presented made them feel as if they weren't working hard enough. This isn't the first time you have questioned the judgement of Barbara, your boss. She certainly is intelligent and hard-working, but she doesn't seem very interested in what's going on out in the field. Furthermore, she doesn't seem very receptive to 'bad news' about sales and customer complaints.

(Note: During this meeting, use the forcing approach to conflict management and negotiations shown in Table 2, page 19. However, don't overplay your part – you are the senior regional sales manager and if Barbara continues to move up quickly in the organisation, you may be in line for her position.)

Skill Application

Application Activities for Managing Conflict

Suggested Further Assignments

1. Select a specific conflict with which you are very familiar. Using the framework for identifying the sources of a conflict, discussed in this book, analyse this situation carefully. It might be useful to compare your perceptions of the situation with those of informed observers. What type of conflict is this? Why did it occur? Why is it continuing? Next, using the guidelines for selecting an appropriate conflict-management strategy, identify the general approach that would be most appropriate for this situation. Consider both the personal preferences of the parties involved and the relevant situational factors. Is this the approach that the parties have been using? If not, attempt to introduce a different perspective into the relationship and explain why you feel it would be more productive. If the parties have been using this approach, discuss with them why it has not been successful thus far. Share information on specific behavioural guidelines (or negotiation tactics) that might increase the effectiveness of their efforts.

2. Identify a situation where another individual is doing something that needs to be corrected. Using the respondent's guidelines for collaborative problem-solving, construct a plan for discussing your concerns with this person. Include specific language designed to assertively state your case without causing a defensive reaction. Role-play this interaction with a friend and incorporate any suggestions for improvement. Make your presentation to the individual and report on your results. What was the reaction? Were you successful in balancing assertiveness with support and responsibility? Based on this experience, identify other situations that you feel need to be changed and follow a similar procedure.

3. Act as a mediator between two individuals or groups. Using the guidelines for implementing the collaborative approach to mediation, outline a plan of action prior to your intervention. Consider whether initial private meetings are appropriate. Report on the

situation and your plan. How did you feel? What specific actions worked well? What was the outcome? What should you have done differently? Based on this experience, revise your plan for use in related situations.

4. Identify a difficult situation involving negotiations. This might involve transactions at work, at home or in the community. Review the guidelines for integrative bargaining and identify the specific tactics you plan to use. Write down specific questions and responses to likely initiatives from the other party. In particular, anticipate how you might handle the possibility of the other party's utilising a distributive negotiation strategy. Schedule a negotiation meeting with the party involved and implement your plan. Following the session, debrief the experience with a co-worker or friend. What did you learn? How successful were you? What would you do differently? Based on this experience, modify your plan and prepare to implement it in related situations.

Application Plan and Evaluation

The objective of this exercise is to help you apply your skills in a real-life setting. Now that you have become familiar with the behavioural guidelines that form the basis of effective skill performance, you will improve the most by trying out those guidelines in an everyday context.

The trouble is, unlike a classroom activity in which feedback is immediate and others can assist you with their evaluations, this skill application activity is one you must accomplish and evaluate on your own. There are two parts to this activity. Part 1 helps prepare you to apply the skill. Part 2 helps you evaluate and improve on your experience. Be sure to actually write down answers to each item. Don't short-circuit the process by skipping steps.

Part 1 – Planning

1. Write down the two or three aspects of this skill that are most important to you. These may be areas of weakness, areas you most want to improve or areas that are most salient to a problem you currently face. Identify the specific aspects of this skill that you want to apply.

2. Now identify the setting or situation in which you will apply this skill. Establish a plan for performance by actually writing down

the situation. Who else will be involved? When will you do it? Where will it be done?

3. What specific behaviours will you engage in to apply this skill. Practise them.

4. What are the indicators of successful performance? How will you know you have succeeded in being effective? What will indicate that you have performed competently?

Part 2 – Evaluation

5. After you have completed your implementation, record the results. What happened? How successful were you? What was the effect on others?

6. How can you improve? What modifications can you make next time? What will you do differently in a similar situation in the future?

7. Looking back on your whole skill practice and application experience, what have you learned? What has been surprising? In what ways might this experience help you in the long term?

Scoring Key

Managing Interpersonal Conflict

To find your score for each skill area, add your rating scores together for the relevant questions.

Skill area	Question numbers	Assessment pre-	post-
Initiating a complaint	1 to 8		
Responding to a criticism	9 to 16	_____	_____
Mediating a conflict	17 to 24	_____	_____
TOTAL SCORE:		_____	_____

To assess how well you scored on this instrument, compare your scores to three comparison standards:

- Compare your score with the maximum possible (144).
- Compare your scores with the scores of other students in your class.
- Compare your scores to a norm group consisting of 500 practising managers and business school students. In comparison to the norm group, if you scored:

    120 or above, you are in the top quartile;

    116 to 119, you are in the second quartile;

    98 to 115, you are in the third quartile;

    97 or below, you are in the bottom quartile.

Strategies for Handling Conflict

	Forcing			Accommodating	
Item	*Score*		*Item*	*Score*	
1	_____		4	_____	
6	_____		9	_____	
11	_____		14	_____	
16	_____		19	_____	
Total	_____		Total	_____	

	Avoiding			Collaborating	
Item	*Score*		*Item*	*Score*	
2	_____		5	_____	
7	_____		10	_____	
12	_____		15	_____	
17	_____		20	_____	
Total	_____		Total	_____	

	Compromising	
Item	*Score*	
3	_____	
8	_____	
13	_____	
18	_____	
Total	_____	

Primary conflict–management strategy: _____
(highest score)

Secondary conflict–management strategy: _____
(next highest score)

Exercises in Selecting an Appropriate Conflict-Management Strategy

Argyll Steakhouse

The various approaches to this situation could be:

■ **Forcing** – This is a non-smoking section. Please tell those people to move into a smoking area to finish their coffee.

■ **Compromising** – I realise that the place is crowded and I don't want a fuss, but could we perhaps be given a table further away from the smokers?

- **Accommodating** – The smoke is getting to my daughter's throat. Please ask them to finish their coffee in the lounge and let us know when the table is clear.
- **Collaborating** – Would it be possible for us to move our table, away from the smoke?
- **Avoiding** – Let's go somewhere else.

The situation constraints are – high issue importance, low relationship importance (although you may wish to go to the Steakhouse again), relative power probably high and time pressures (even though your son has taken his sister away from the smoke) medium high – its a cold night. The Forcing alternative is probably the best choice. Forcing can of course be sole and does not need to be founded on aggression.

Proceed to tackle the next two assignments, Avocado Computer and Phelan Ltd, in a similar way.

Observer's Feedback Form

Resolving Interpersonal Disputes

Where's My Speech?, Can Harry Fit In? Hartford Manufacturing Company

ACTION	RATING (1=low, 5=high)
Initiator	
Maintained personal ownership of the problem, including feelings	___
Avoided making accusations or attributing motives	___
Succinctly described the problem (behaviours, outcomes, feelings)	___
Specified expectations or standards violated	___
Persisted until understood	___
Encouraged two-way interaction	___
Approached multiple issues incrementally (proceeded from simple to complex, easy to hard)	___
Appealed to what the disputants had in common (goals, principles, constraints)	___
Made a specific request for change	___

Respondent

Showed genuine concern and interest

Responded appropriately to the initiator's emotions ___

Avoided becoming defensive or overreacting ___

Sought additional information about the problem (shifted general to specific, evaluative to descriptive) ___

Focused on one issue at a time, gradually broadening the scope of the discussion, searching for an integrative solution ___

Agreed with some aspect of the complaint (facts, perceptions, feelings or principles) ___

Asked for suggestions for making changes ___

Proposed a specific plan of action ___

Mediator (where a mediator has been used)

Treated the conflict and disputants seriously

Broke down complex issues, separated the critical from the peripheral. ___

Began with a relatively easy problem ___

Helped disputants avoid entrenched positions by exploring underlying interests ___

Remained neutral (facilitator, not judge) ___

Pointed out the effect of the conflict on performance ___

Kept the interaction issue-oriented ___

Made sure that neither party dominated the conversation ___

Kept conflict in perspective by emphasising areas of agreement ___

Helped generate multiple alternatives ___

Made sure that both parties were satisfied and committed to the proposed resolution ___

Comments:

Glossary

Accommodating approach	A response to conflict that tries to preserve a friendly interpersonal relationship by satisfying the other party's concerns while ignoring one's own. It generally produces a lose-lose situation to nobody's satisfaction.
Altruistic-nurturing personality	A type of personality that seeks gratification through the promotion of harmony and the enhancement of the welfare of others without expecting any reward.
Analytic-autonomising personality	A type of personality that seeks gratification through the achievement of self-sufficiency, self reliance and logical orderliness.
Assertive–directing personality	The type of personality that seeks gratification through self assertion and directs the activities of others with the expectation of reward.
Avoiding response	An unassertive, uncooperative reaction to conflict that neglects the interests of both parties by side-stepping the issue. The resultant frustration may cause a power struggle as others rush in to fill the vacuum.
Brainstorming	A technique designed to help problem-solving by generating volumes of alternatives in a positive atmosphere.
Broken record	A technique of Assertiveness Training where a core objective is isolated and repeated until accepted by a respondent.
Collaborating response	The cooperative, assertive, problem-solving way of solving conflict. It focuses on finding solutions to the basic problems and issues that are acceptable to both parties, rather than on finding fault of allocating blame. Of the conflict management strategies, this is the only true win-win approach.
Compromising response	A reaction to conflict that attempts to find satisfaction for both parties by 'splitting the difference'. If over used, it sends the message that settling disputes is more important than solving problems.
Conflict	Disagreement between individuals functional or dyfunctional at any level from mild disapproval to 'open' warfare.
Distributive negotiation strategies	An approach that requires both parties to sacrifice something to resolve the conflict by dividing a fixed 'cake'.

Dysfunctional conflict	Conflict that does not have a productive output.
Fielding	A technique of Assertiveness Training, often coupled with Broken Record where the respondent acknowledges the words of the initiator by repeating them in some form but not necessarily acknowledging their complete truth or relevance.
Forcing response	An assertive, uncooperative response to conflict that uses the exercise of authority to satisfy one's own needs at the expense of another's.
Human Resource Director (HRM)	This title is a result of the newly perceived role of 'personnel management' in organisations. The new status of HRM is that of an integrating and integrated function within an organisation.
Integrative negotiation strategies	An approach in which the focus is on collaborative ways of 'expanding the cake' by avoiding fixed, incompatible positions.
Supportive communication	Communication that helps others share information accurately and honestly without putting in question medium- and long-term relationships.
Process	How things are done as opposed to what is done. In discussing interpersonal skills, process is seen as the way a task is performed by individuals and groups.

References

Adler, R. B. *Satisfying personal needs: Managing conflicts, making requests, and saying no. Confidence in communication: A guide to assertive and social skills.* New York: Holt, Rinehart & Winston, 1977.

Argenti, J. *Corporate Collapse: The causes and symptoms.* New York: Wiley, 1976.

Bazerman, M. Why negotiations go wrong. *Psychology Today*, June 1986, 54–58.

Belbin, M. *Management teams.* Heinemann, 1981.

Boulding, E. Further reflections on conflict management. In R. L. Kahn & E. Boulding (Eds.), *Power and conflict in organizations.* New York: Basic Books, 1964.

Cameron, Kim S., Kim, Myung U. & Whetten, David A. Organizational effects of decline and turbulence. *Administrative Science Quarterly*, 1987, 32, 222–240.

Cummings, L. L., Harnett, D. L. & Stevens, O. J. Risk, fate, conciliation and trust: An international study of attitudinal differences among executives. *Academy of Management Journal*, 1971, 14, 285–304.

Do mergers really work? *Business Week*, June 3, 1985, 88–100.

Filley, A. C. Some normative issues in conflict management. *California Management Review*, 1978, 71, 61–66.

Filley, A. C. *Interpersonal conflict resolution.* Glenview, Ill.: Scott Foresman, 1975.

Fisher, R. & Brown, S. *Getting together: Building a relationship that gets to yes.* London: Hutchinson, 1988.

Fortune, 23 July, 1984, 74.

Gordon, W. J. J. *Synectics: the development of creative capacity.* Harper and Row: New York, 1961.

Hines, J. S. *Conflict and conflict management.* Athens, Ga.: University of Georgia Press, 1980.

How to make confrontation work for you. *Fortune*, 23 July, 1984, 73–75.

Kelly, J. Make conflict work for you. *Harvard Business Review*, July–August 1970, 48, 103–113.

King, D. Three cheers for conflict. *Personnel*, 1981, 48, 13–22.

Kipnis, D. & Schmidt, S. An influence perspective in bargaining within organizations. In M. H. Bazerman & R. J. Lewicki (Eds.), *Bargaining inside organizations.* Beverly Hills, Calif.: Sage Publications, 1983.

Latham, G. & Wexley, K. *Increasing productivity through performance appraisal*. Reading, Mass.: Addison-Wesley, 1981.

Maslow, A. *Eupsychian Management*. Homewood, Ill.: Irwin, 1965.

Morris, W. & Sashkin, M. *Organizational behavior in action*. St. Paul, Minn: West Publishing, 1976.

Northcraft, G. & Neale, M. *Organization Behavior*. Chicago: Dryden Press, 1990.

Phillips, E. & Cheston, R. Conflict resolution: What works. *California Management Review*, 1979, 21, 76-83.

Porter, E. H. *Manual of administration and interpretation for strength deployment inventory*. LaJolla, Calif.: Personal Strengths Assessment Service, 1973.

Pruitt, D. G. Integrative agreements: Nature and consequences. In M. H. Bazerman & R. J. Lewicki, (Eds.), *Negotiating in Organizations*. Beverly Hills. Calif.: Sage Publishing, 1983.

Robbins, S. P. Conflict management and conflict resolution are not synonymous terms. *California Management Review*, 1978, 21, 67-75.

Robbins, S. P. *Managing organizational conflict: A nontraditional approach*. Englewood Cliffs, N.J.: Prentice-Hall, 1974.

Ruble, T. & Thomas, K. Support for a two-dimensional model of conflict behavior. *Organizational Behavior and Human Performance*, 1976, 16, 145.

Savage, G. T., Blair, J. D. & Sorenson, R. L. Consider both relationships and substance when negotiating strategically. *Academy of Management Executive*, 1989, 3, 37-48.

Schmidt, W. H. & Tannenbaum, R. Management of differences. *Harvard Business Review*, Nov.-Dec. 1965, 38, 107-115.

Schriesheim, C. & VonGlinow, M. The path-goal theory of leadership: A theoretical and empirical analysis. *Academy of Management Journal*, 1977, 20, 398-405.

Smith, W. P. Conflict and negotiation: Trends and emerging issues. *Journal of Applied Social Psychology*, 1987, 17, 631-677.

Thomas, K. Conflict and conflict management. In M. D. Dunnette (Ed.), *Handbook of industrial and organizational psychology*. London: Routledge and Kegan Paul, 1976.

Thomas, K. W. Toward multi-dimensional values in teaching: The example of conflict behavior. *Academy of Management Review*, 1977, 2, 487.

Walton, R. *Interpersonal peacekeeping: Confrontations and third party consultation*. Reading, Mass.: Addison-Wesley, 1969.

Wanous, J. P. & Youtz, A. Solution diversity and the quality of group decisions. *Academy of Management Journal*, 1986, 1, 149-159.

Woods, M. *The Aware Manager*. Element books: Shaftesbury, 1989.

Index